HALL OF FAITH SERIES

God's Warrior of Vanuatu

WALTER SCRAGG and NANCY IRLAND

Pacific Press Publishing Association
Boise, Idaho
Oshawa, Ontario, Canada

Edited by Marvin Moore
Designed by Consuelo Udave
Cover art by Jim Padgett
Type set in 10/12 Century Schoolbook

Library of Congress Catalog Number: 88-63386

ISBN 0-8163-0825-X

89 90 91 92 93 • 5 4 3 2 1

Contents

Chapter 1
Murder in the Jungle

It was another morning that would end in murder.

The dark-skinned mother awoke to the sound of thunder. Lightning ripped the sky. The monsoon rains thrashing the jungle vegetation filled her senses until she felt as though this sound was all she would ever hear. She turned over lazily, as she always did in the morning, to snuggle her baby and feed him before the day began. Already, her husband was up—hunting, no doubt.

Mary lived with her husband Ool in the jungle village of Bartarmul. Bartarmul was nestled in a range of mountains that ran along the coast of Malekula, a volcanic island in the New Hebrides. Mary's baby's name was Dick.[1]

Mary pulled Dick closer to her side, fingering the soft ringlets on his head and watching his tiny chest rise and fall in rhythm. Normally he looked up at her and opened his mouth in a tiny yawn whenever she awakened him, but this morning she realized with a start that something was different. He was much too quiet. He was much too warm. He lay beside her like a burning log. Just five months old, the baby usually demanded to be fed often through the night. But he had slept throughout this past night, and he still slept. Had he awakened and she had not heard him because of the rain? That was impossible!

Fear shot through Mary's mind. She had seen other babies die

---

[1]Mary was not the woman's real name, though it might have been. From the time that white traders first visited the New Hebrides, the islanders began adopting English names for their children. The baby's name was Dick.

quietly like this. When baby girls got sick, their mothers were expected to abandon them in the jungle. Mary shuddered, remembering the baby girls she'd seen who died at the mercy of the wilds—or of headhunters. But what was she to do with a sick baby boy? Why hadn't she asked more questions of the other mothers? What had she done to deserve this punishment from the gods? She wouldn't let the boar gods take her baby son!

Mary scrambled to her feet, wondering what to do. She must wake him up! Bouncing the baby in her arms, she called to him, walking back and forth inside the small hut trying to avoid the streams of water pouring in from the roof, trying not to slip on the mud, trying to keep her baby from dying. What else could she do? Would Ool allow her to take the baby to the white men down near the coast? Other women had, but without the men's knowledge.

A sudden bawling at the door arrested Mary's attention. More troubles: Ool's favorite boar stood at the low end of the thatched dwelling, shaking water from its back. It was an ugly animal, with tusks that curled in a complete circle on each side of its face. Yet Ool thought this pig was beautiful!

In Bartarmul, a man showed his wealth and status by the number of pigs he owned. Ool had many pigs. He was second in command in the village, next to the chief. Only he and the chief were allowed to own a tusked boar, and this was Ool's prized one. Soon he would display it to the other villagers and receive the honor the boar would bring. It was almost like owning a real god. It was a woman's prime responsibility to care for her husband's boars, to keep them safely inside the fence at the low, front end of the house.

The boar shook again, and water sprayed all over the front part of the hut. In that instant Mary forgot all about Dick, for she realized that the boar had gotten out into the rain. She hurried to the boar with a sharp cry, hoping she could dry it off before her husband found out. How could she have been so careless as to allow her concern for her baby to distract her from her first responsibility of caring for the pig?

Ool was a short man—barely four feet tall—but he had a mean temper. He had a reputation for killing people who angered him.

Unfortunately, this morning Mary was too slow. Ool's dark

body shadowed the door. He looked down at the boar, and a low growl escaped from deep in his throat and exploded into a shout. "You fool! My boar is wet!"

Mary bowed toward him, holding up the baby. "I'm sorry—your son is not well. I was caring for him and—"

Ool strode toward her, his club upraised. Now she could see his matted beard and his sharply beaked nose. Oh, how she feared him!

"You are useless to me!" Ool shouted, his eyes blazing red with rage. "You can't even take care of a pig properly!" With an angry shout, he hurled the club at his wife. It struck her on the head with a dull thud.

The club fell to the muddy floor, and with a small cry the woman, too, collapsed, clutching her baby in her arms.

Ool stared at her with cold eyes, expecting her to open her eyes and say something to him, but she didn't move. She lay quietly in the cold mud with her eyes closed. A trickle of blood stained her dark forehead as it ran slowly into her black, curly hair. When he saw her grip on the baby loosen, he knew that she was dead. He kicked her leg just to make sure. She did not move. Ool had seen people die before. It did not bother him.

He left her there and went over to care for his prized boar. He was not sorry. Boars were more important than women! Her life would not be wasted. Her body would bring a fine price in a neighboring village for stew meat.

Suddenly he remembered that she had said his son was not well! His wife he did not care about, but his son—that was someone he prized as much as his pigs!

Ool stooped to take the baby from its mother's lifeless arms. He was startled at the warmth of the baby's body. Dick opened his eyes and began to cry. Crying irritated Ool. Dick's crying was so loud that he could scarcely hear the rain. Suddenly Ool was faced with a whole new set of problems: Who would feed the baby? Who would cook for him? More important, who would care for his pigs?

The downpour ended as quickly as it had begun. Ool clutched the baby to his chest and hurried to the hut next door. Chickens clucked and scurried underfoot as he pushed his way inside, past the pigs, to a woman at the rear of the hut, where the roof was higher. She was stirring a pot of food.

The woman did not welcome him. Men were feared in that village. She eyed Ool cautiously and asked, "What do you want?"

"My wife is dead," Ool said. "She was not a good woman. She did not care for my pigs properly, so I killed her. Now I need someone to feed my baby."

"Why should I care for your baby?" the woman snorted. "It's not my fault that his mother is dead. You killed her. You can kill her baby. His flesh must be very tender!"

Ool felt his anger begin to rise. With a shout, he laid the baby down, raced over to a small stack of firewood in the corner, and picked up a stout stick. Grabbing the woman by one arm, he beat her to death in front of her screaming children. "More meat for the next village," he thought to himself.

Wiping his hands, Ool picked up the baby and stalked out of the hut, oblivious to the cries of the children inside. He had to find someone to take care of his prized son! Trudging through the muddy village with the baby in his arms, Ool decided who that person would be. He would demand that his wife's youngest sister, Lehtari, move in with him and care for Dick. It was the custom in Bartarmul that sisters take care of each other's children. Not quite thirteen, and never having had a baby of her own, Lehtari would not have milk for Dick. She would have to find a friend with a baby who would nurse Ool's baby too.

Ool smiled smugly. Lehtari was of marriageable age. He could part with a couple of pigs in payment for her. Then she would *have* to care for his son.

Chapter 2
Running Away

Lehtari struggled to be a good wife to Ool, but she was terribly frightened of what he might do to her if she failed in any way. Fortunately, Dick recovered within a few days under the care of an experienced mother in the village who was nursing two other babies at the time.

One day, seven months later, Lehtari struggled up the dirt path from the beach with a load of driftwood balanced on her head and Dick tied to her back. At one year he still wasn't very heavy, but Lehtari was not very big herself. She was thirteen years old and already a stepmother!

She had lived with Ool seven months now. His influence in the village was weakening as a result of his temper, and he was beginning to mellow. He was still a fine cannibal warrior, but cannibals were not supposed to kill people of their own village! They killed for "noble" reasons, like property disputes with neighboring villages, commands of the gods, and things like that. Also, the killing of neighboring villagers was a good way to obtain meat. Ool would rather eat human flesh than kill a sacred animal for food—especially a pig!

Ool's friends no longer came to him for advice the way they used to. As a result, Ool was quiet more often. He took a silent pride in his herd of pigs, but nobody seemed interested in his prize hog—the one whose wanderings had resulted in his wife's murder. He never displayed the hog at ceremonial feasts anymore.

Lehtari paused to adjust the weight of the baby on her bare back. He was so heavy when he went to sleep! Standing alone in the shadows of the mountain path that seemed literally cut out of the side of the mountain, she glanced out over the wide expanse of crystal blue water in the bay and caught her breath sharply. A great black ship made its way into Malua Bay. Lehtari knew what would happen next. The ship would make a thunderous noise, and the villagers would scurry down to the beach for free passage to Australia where they would work as slaves in the white men's sugarcane fields. If the villagers who volunteered to go were not enough, others would be kidnapped and taken anyway. Many villagers who were kidnapped never came back.

Because of his disgrace in the village, Ool had been hinting that he wanted to leave. Once he told her that he wanted to take her and Dick to Australia. She might never see her family again!

Lehtari shuddered, but despite the fear in her heart, she hurried along the path toward the village. She must make Ool feel content with life where they were, on Malekula Island. She must make a feast for their evening meal and do the best she could to talk him out of leaving!

Lehtari heard the boom a few minutes later as she left the shadows of the jungle and entered the village clearing. Naked chickens, their feathers plucked for headdresses, squawked and fluttered into the huts nearby. A herd of frightened wild pigs crashed through the underbrush, snorting and squealing. Dick awoke. He stiffened in the cloth on Lehtari's back, and then he began to cry. His screams joined the cries of other naked children running through the village.

Lehtari's own heart raced. She passed by the chief's "skull house" quickly. She hated to see those human skulls hanging from poles. They reminded her that someday warriors from a neighboring village would again raid Bartarmul, and her skull might hang from another chief's hut! Reaching her own hut, she entered through the low side and hurried past the pigs to the back. There she could stand up and slip the baby off her shoulders with one hand while guiding the driftwood to the dirt floor with the other.

Keeping one eye on Dick, who played quietly with a squeaking baby pig, Lehtari stirred up the fire and began preparing the evening meal. Ool would bring some fresh human meat in a basket. She could prepare it quickly, and then she would try to talk him out of leaving.

Another cannon blast rent the jungle silence. Seagulls screamed, and Lehtari's heart screamed with them. "I don't want to go!" she moaned silently. "I don't want Ool to take me away!"

Hurrying through the jungle quietly, Ool patted the pouch of poison-tipped arrows that hung at his side. He was a good shot. If the butcher at the next village did not have any low-class people for him to kill, he would choose one for himself—maybe even the butcher! It didn't matter to Ool.

Then he heard the cannon. A ship was in the bay! He knew that it wouldn't be there long. He must hurry to Bartarmul and command Lehtari to collect their things. He had heard that those who went willingly were promised safe passage back to Malekula after three or four years of working in Australia. Ool wanted to get away. He wanted to see how the white men lived. Like it or not, Lehtari and the baby were going with him to Australia!

Chapter 3
Encounter With Cannibals

Ool's back glistened under the burning sun, and his muscles rippled as he hacked away at the tall sugarcane stalks towering twice his own height. The leaves were rough as a cat's tongue and tore at his hands. He bundled the stalks and carried them over his shoulder to the cart that would take them to the factory. Young Dick, now five years old, played nearby, sucking the sweet juice from short, fibery portions of sugarcane that his father had cut off for him.

Ool was proud of his boy! Lehtari shared Ool's pride in Dick's bright eyes and bubbling personality. And the questions he asked! How were they to know the answers? They were as unfamiliar with the white men's way of life as Dick was! Even though houses with white man's furniture were provided for the workers, Lehtari and Ool preferred to sleep on the floor on their mats, as they were accustomed to do. But Dick often curled up on the bed. "It doesn't hurt my bones!" he would explain with a smile.

They had been moved from plantation to plantation, following the sugarcane harvest. Now they were on the island of Aore.[1] Soon their time working for the white man would be over, and they would return to Bartarmul on the island of Malekula. Lehtari could hardly wait, but Ool worried. How would Dick fit in with village life when they returned to Bartarmul at the end of the month? There was so much to teach his son about their heritage, especially about the way of the Big Nambus—the fierc-

---

[1]Aore is actually one of the islands of the New Hebrides where Ool and Lahteri had come from, but they were still fulfilling their contract for the white man.

est, most savage tribe on the volcanic island of Malekula. Big Nambus were identified by the big loincloths the men wore around their waists. Little Nambus wore smaller loincloths. The loincloth was an important thing to look for before shooting a poisoned arrow!

But Dick was bright. He would learn quickly. Perhaps someday he would even be chief of Bartarmul!

Bartarmul. Ool smiled as he remembered the village. He would take another wife, and he would hunt again. Ool and Lehtari had not tasted human flesh for four years now, and Ool missed it. It would be easier to prepare with the bush knife he had acquired from working on the plantations. It would be good to be home again!

But when they arrived back home, Ool and Lehtari found that things had changed on the island of Malekula. White men calling themselves "missionaries" were again living in the houses on Malua Bay. They had come to Malua Bay many years before. Ool had passed by their neat little huts, and he remembered hearing stories about them from villagers who had had dealings with them. Ool remembered hearing his father tell how he had killed a white missionary. In time, the missionaries had left, but now they were back. This new family had moved in just after Ool and Lehtari went to Australia, and it was obvious to Ool that they had been trying to change things on the island during the entire four years that he was gone.

As far as Ool was concerned, it was all because of old Nehambat, an ancient chief of the largest Big Nambus village. He told such a strange story! It had happened many years before—even before the first white missionary came to Malekula.

Nehambat was tired, so he lay down on his mat early that night and was soon fast asleep. How long he slept he could not say. He heard no noise, but suddenly a blinding light woke him up. He clapped a hand over his eyes, and then slowly removed it as his eyes adjusted to the intense brightness. What he saw made him gasp. A bright shining being stood before him—a being like a man, yet much larger than any man he had ever seen, and with a much more commanding appearance.

At first Nehambat was terrified and speechless. This must be the great white spirit that his father had told him about, and that his father's father had told him about But the white spirit just stood there. Realizing that this fantastic personage meant him no harm, Nehambat finally found words to speak. "Who are you? What do you want?"

"I am an angel," the being said. "I have come to tell you that you and your villagers must make many changes."

"What kind of changes must we make?" Nehambat asked in surprise.

"You must leave the island and search for someone to come and teach you what to do," the angel said.

"But how will I know who the teacher is?" Nehambat asked.

The angel held up a black book. "The teacher will instruct you from this book. Go now, and find him."

Wide awake by now, the old chief studied the dark thatched walls of his hut. He pinched himself. It *was* real, wasn't it? The great white spirit had spoken to him. He must obey

Before the sun came up, Nehambat gathered up his headdress and slathered himself with a fresh coat of pig grease and ashes for warmth. Then he made his way stealthily down the mountain trail to the lagoon. There, he paid a fisherman to take him to the islands of New Caledonia.

The streets of Nouméa were not very crowded. Nehambat strode confidently through town, searching every man's face and hands, looking for the black book he had seen in his dream. To his dismay, he never saw it. But near the end of the day he heard a voice. It was not the voice of someone talking to him. The sound did not come through his ears, yet he heard it just as clearly as though it had. "The man coming toward you now is the one you are looking for," the voice said.

Nehambat looked up. Sure enough, a man was approaching. He stopped walking and waited. As the man passed by, he grabbed his arm. "You must come to visit the Big Nambus of Malekula in the mountains of the western coast," Nehambat said.

The man looked at him without speaking, and Nehambat studied his face pleadingly. Then, feeling confident that he had fulfilled his mission, Nehambat turned, walked back to the shore, and paid another fisherman to paddle him back to Malekula.

For ten years, Nehambat waited for the man to come.

One day as Lilingeto, Nehambat's cousin, was fishing in a

lagoon[2] he heard a noise coming from the open sea. Turning, he saw a small boat putter into the lagoon and anchor offshore. A white man jumped over the side and waded toward him.

"G'day!" the white man called, smiling.

The chief 's cousin said nothing. He pulled himself up as tall as he could, noting with some concern that he came only to the white man's elbows.

The white man repeated his greeting in what he hoped was the islander's language. "I am Pastor Parker," he said, holding up his Bible. "I want to see the high chief. You will show me?"

"It takes many hours to walk through the mountains," Lilingeto told Pastor Parker. "But I will show you the way."

"Thank you!" Pastor Parker gestured for Lilingeto to lead the way. Lilingeto struck off through the jungle, and Pastor Parker followed as well as he could. There was hardly a trail through the deep forest. Jungle birds called a warning overhead, and monkeys screamed at each other from the treetops, shaking the branches as they swung from vine to vine. One particular birdcall caught Pastor Parker's attention. Each time Lilingeto heard it, he looked to the sides and behind him at Pastor Parker.

The pastor whispered a prayer, asking for God's protection.

All at once they were surrounded by native men with necklaces of human teeth around their necks. Lilingeto spoke to them in a dialect the pastor did not understand. Lilingeto eyed Pastor Parker from head to toe. Suddenly one of the others sprang toward Pastor Parker, tied his hands behind his back, and threw him to the ground. Pastor Parker realized that he had been double-crossed! Lilingeto had led him into a trap!

Tom-toms began to beat, calling the chief and his attendants down the mountain for a cannibalistic feast. The islanders began to dance and chant. Pastor Parker whispered a quick prayer and struggled to get up, but it was useless. His hands were bound too tightly. What could he do? Suddenly he remembered a flashlight that he carried in his pocket. Maybe he could "buy his way" out of this predicament!

---

[2]In the islands of the South Pacific, a lagoon is not a pond on land but rather a large area of water near the island that is encircled by a coral reef.

Squirming on the ground, he managed to get the flashlight out of his pocket and call the people's attention to it. The chanting stopped, but the tom-toms continued their driving beat. Holding the flashlight behind his back, Pastor Parker turned it on and off. The people gasped, and each of them took a turn turning the light off and on and shining it into the forest. They chattered with each other, amazed at this object's miraculous power to produce light.

Pastor Parker prayed, asking God to spare his life.

Soon, however, the cannibals tired of the flashlight and resumed their preparations for "Parker stew." They dragged the pastor toward a large sharp stone nearby. Pastor Parker realized that they planned to kill him by cracking his head open on the stone. He continued to struggle. Just when he feared that it was all over, he heard a shout from behind.

Nehambat approached the group with blazing eyes. Apparently, when the men first encountered Pastor Parker, they found his Bible and wrenched it from his hands, and the chief had found it lying beside the trail. This was the black book he had been waiting to see! This was the man the angel had promised would come! He had been waiting ten years to see this man!

Nehambat raised the pastor's Bible and shook it at his men. The tom-toms were silenced. "What do you think you are doing?" Nehambat bellowed. "This is the missionary who has come to teach us. This is the book the white spirit showed me!" He stalked around the group, scolding them. "You cannot hurt this man! Untie his hands and let him speak. I have been waiting for him."

The cannibals murmured and untied the pastor's hands. Nehambat handed him his Bible. "Speak," he said. "Tell us what we must do to change our ways." Crossing his arms, he sat down on the rock which, moments before, was to have been the pastor's butcher block. He motioned for the others to be seated as well.

With a sigh of relief and a prayer of thanks, Pastor Parker opened his Bible and told the people about the love of Jesus. He explained that Jesus wanted people to live together in harmony, respecting human life. He told them about heaven and the second coming. He saw the chief listening in rapt attention. At last he closed his eyes and prayed aloud. Then he tucked his Bible under his arm and prepared to leave.

Chief Nehambat jumped up and grabbed his arm. Pastor

Parker's heart lurched. Was he going to become stew in a cannibal's pot after all?

"You cannot go," the chief said.

"But I must go," Pastor Parker replied.

"I will not let you go unless you promise to come back and tell us more about this man Jesus. Others in my village must hear these stories." Nehambat looked into the pastor's face. The odor of his unwashed body burned the pastor's nostrils.

Pastor Parker nodded. "I will return," he promised.

With that assurance, Nehambat stepped aside so he could pass, while Nehambat's men silently vanished into the forest.

Pastor Parker returned to his mission station on the small nearby island of Aitchin. Two times he returned to Malekula before leaving on furlough to Australia. But for some reason he never got to the village of Bartarmul where Ool and his family lived.

While in Australia, Pastor Parker presented many mission stories in various churches and told of his close brush with death. "The Big Nambus are some of the most savage, bloodthirsty cannibals in the New Hebrides," he said. "They, especially, need to know of God's love. Is there anyone who will answer God's call and say, 'I will go. I will show these people God's plan for them. I will show them a better way of life'?"

Norman and Alma Wiles were moved. They had wanted to be missionaries, and this seemed like the challenge they had been waiting for. The next year they decided to take the story of Jesus to the cannibals of Malekula. Norman was an Australian. Alma's parents were Americans who had sailed from America on the *Pitcairn*, and settled in Australia. Norman and Alma were young and filled with enthusiasm. It was an adventure that would change their lives forever.

The day they arrived on the island of Malekula was a day that Alma would never forget. She stood on the bow of their small boat, watching the lush, palm-studded island grow closer and closer. When at last Norman anchored the boat and jumped out, Alma pulled up her skirts and reached for his outstretched hand. He smiled reassuringly as she stepped over the side of the boat beside him into the warm, shallow water.

"Welcome to Malua Bay," he said with a bow. In a wide,

sweeping gesture, he asked, "And where would you like to build your new house, my dear? It is not very crowded, as you can see—you can have your pick of the neighborhood!"

Alma chuckled. Then she gripped Norman's arm and gasped. An assembly of fierce savages appeared silently at the edge of the forest, unsmiling and unmoving, standing like guards. "They don't want us here," Alma whispered.

"Pray," Norman whispered back. He smiled and held up his hands to show he was unarmed. "G'day! We have come because of Chief Nehambat's invitation."

The savages did not return the smile. Unknown to the Wiles the Big Nambus were in a particularly bloodthirsty mood. A British warship had just shelled one of their villages a few days before in retaliation for a native headhunting expedition

Then Pastor Wiles held up his Bible. When the savages saw the Bible, they melted back into the jungle just as silently as they had come, and left the missionaries alone.

A small hut was soon standing near the bay. From that mission outpost, Pastor and Mrs. Wiles trekked into the mountain villages offering medical care and Bible stories to those islanders who were brave enough or desperate enough to come to them. But they never came to Ool's village of Bartarmul.

However, in the villages where they did visit, the people came to accept them as friends. A few of the more desperate villagers even sought their medical treatments, and always, along with the medicine, Norman and Alma dispensed the stories of God's love.

But living in the jungle was not easy on the missionaries. Vicious malarial mosquitoes attacked them, and they became deathly ill with dysentery. After just a few years on Malekula, they were forced to return to Australia to recover.

While they were gone, the Big Nambus returned to their old ways. Savage fighting broke out between the Big Nambus tribes. The people were killing and eating each other.

Hearing of this, and knowing that the friends they had made in the villages were in grave danger, Norman and Alma decided to return to their jungle home despite the fact that they had not yet fully recovered. They wanted to help the people mediate their differences. Again they left the comfortable life in Australia and settled into their jungle hut. Norman trekked to the major Nambus village and called meetings of the tribal chiefs, helping them to mediate their differences. Again he earned their respect.

But when he returned to the mission hut, Norman was shivering with cold in spite of the heat, and burning up with a fever. Alma was worried. She was not well herself. Working with these cannibals seemed so futile! Would they never change and become Christians? She and Norman had been witnessing to them for more than eight years, and not one cannibal had asked to become a Christian! It was hard not to feel discouraged. Often she had seen the very people who knew better pass her house with baskets on their heads, a human hand sticking out of the top, and she knew that another killing had taken place. Soon she heard the drum of the tom-toms, and she knew that another cannibal feast was in the making.

Just a few days after Norman had returned from his journey into the jungle, word came through one of the messenger women that new fighting had broken out.

Alma studied her husband's drawn face. "You can't go," she said helplessly, knowing that he would anyway.

"I must go, Alma," Norman replied. "I cannot rest knowing that they are killing and eating each other a short distance from here, and knowing that I might have prevented it!"

Despite his fever, Norman dressed and made his way back up to the village for a conference. He persuaded the villagers to stop fighting, and they did—for a while. But Norman had exhausted himself in this seemingly futile work. Two days after he returned home, Norman died of a fatal form of malaria known as blackwater fever.

Alma was alone. The people who lived around the little mission station on the coast deserted her, afraid that they would die next.

Alma bent over her beloved husband's body. With tears streaming down her cheeks, she covered him and said a prayer. Then she picked up a shovel and went outside to dig a grave, but she was too weak, both from grief and from the sickness that also ravaged her body. She looked across the water helplessly, and then she gasped. Was this a vision? She saw a small cutter near the coast and signaled for help. Would they come?

To her relief, three natives set out in a little canoe to help her. They were strangers, but since they were the only other people around, Alma had to trust them. She took them inside and showed them Norman's body. "Please carry him to the top of the small hill outside. I must bury him, but I cannot dig a grave."

When this was done, the natives stepped back as Alma repeated a Scripture verse, offered a prayer, and committed Norman's body to God's care. Dropping a fragrant jungle flower on the grave, she returned to the little mission hut that Norman had built and closed the door for the last time. Then she left with the men who had come to her aid.

It was late on a Friday afternoon when Alma left Malekula Island. As darkness came, a storm began to rage. The men gave up trying to steer the boat through the driving rain and wind. Alma clung to the sides as the little craft tossed about like a matchstick in the surf. She closed her eyes and let the seaspray and rainwater blow into her mouth. Her hair whipped around her face like tiny stinging vines.

Suddenly she felt the boat scrape the bottom, and then the men were pulling her from the boat, urging her to find refuge on the shore. Leaving her there, they returned to the open sea.

Alma was too weak to call after them. She stood alone along the shore of a hostile jungle—bereaved, exhausted, soaking wet, and in total darkness. Finding a cluster of palm trees, she collapsed behind them with her back to the wind and waited for the storm to blow over.

She awoke to silence. The moon was out, sparkling on the now-calm waters. There was no boat in sight. Alma choked back a sob and stood weakly, wondering what to do. Ahead of her, a path led into the jungle. With the moon to guide her, she followed the path. She knew that being a woman, she was fairly safe from savage attack. Women were the lowest class in the villages. Their capture or even death meant no glory to the warrior, so they were usually left alone. Because of this, the messengers sent between warring tribes were usually women. Alma's gravest danger was from wild boars and poisonous snakes.

Miraculously, she tramped the mountain trails for several hours unharmed, until she came to a village on the narrow strait that separated the island of Malekula from Aitchin. The people in that village knew who she was. She rested a while in their village and then signaled the missionaries across the strait to come and pick her up. From there, she returned to Australia alone, wondering if the savages for whom her husband had given his life would ever change their ways.

Chapter 4
Secret Rites

For three years, the mission outpost at Malua Bay stood empty, and the savages returned to their old ways.

Ool delighted in teaching his son the ways of the village. His people seemed to have forgotten their prejudices against him. According to custom, he inherited a position of importance next to the chief as spokesman for the village of Bartarmul. Ool was now called the "talking chief."

As his oldest son, Dick must learn the ways of the village, for when Ool died, Dick would inherit the esteemed position of "talking chief." When he was twelve, Dick and a number of other young boys were taken away for several weeks to attend an initiation school run by the village elders. These secret huts, hidden away from women and small children, held the mysteries of their heathen worship. They believed that magic and spirit worship controlled the crops, fishing, war, the birth of children, the trading of pigs—every facet of life. A man could never grow rich, or remain rich, unless he practiced the right magic and made the right arrangements with the spirits.

In these secret huts Dick was introduced to the boar god, Bheres. He learned secrets of male life from the older men of the village. In time, he would learn how to converse with the skulls, how to call the spirits to his aid, and how to worship the boar god in the right way.

One morning many weeks after he had returned home, Dick awoke to the sound of beating tom-toms reverberating through the hills. He listened carefully to decipher the beat. From his initiation school, he had learned the various rhythms and their meanings—a sort of "jungle message system." A chill went through him as he realized that the drums were beating out the news of impending death. He wanted to go. He wanted to be a part of this ceremony.

"May I go?" he pleaded with his father, jumping up from his mat and running a hand through his dusty hair.

Ool busied himself tying his knife in a hidden pocket in his loincloth and considered the boy's request. He was a bright boy. Perhaps the time had come for him to receive the strength and spirit of a departing warrior. Ool nodded silently and motioned for the boy to follow him out the low door of the hut. Once outside, Ool smeared Dick's body with pig grease and ashes to protect him from the morning's chill. He plucked several feathers from a young chicken's tail and then went back inside the hut to pull out some of Lehtari's hair to weave a headdress for Dick. There wasn't time to make it very fancy, but they could add feathers as they found them on their way.

The dusty trail was dappled with shadows. Dick kept his eyes alert for parrot feathers along the jungle floor. He found several that were brilliant shades of turquoise, green, and red, and pressed them into the still-soft mixture of grease and ashes on his head.

As they neared the place of death, Ool found a long feather from a bird of paradise and held it out with a grin. It was the crowning touch to Dick's headdress.

The songs of the birds were drowned out by the steady, unrelenting beat of the drums. It was all they could hear. The roar was all around them, shaking the dirt under their feet and echoing off the trees. Dick was dizzy with excitement. The hypnotic beat of the drums coursed through his veins. A moment later they broke out of the jungle into a clearing. A large group of men, all of them from Bartarmul, were dancing in a circle. Dick observed with pride that he was one of the youngest boys to attend this ritual. Most of the others were older than he.

A dying warrior lay on the ground in the center of the circle, a vine twisted around his neck. At a signal from the chief, the men began to chant and dance around the man until their greasy bodies were covered with dust. As the dancing continued, their chests heaved with exhaustion, each dry mouth open, gulping air like dying fish.

Dick danced behind his father in a line on one side of the

dying man. Others took their places on the other side. With the beat of the drums in their ears, they all bent down and grasped the vine, lifting it to waist level, testing their grip. Then, with a shout, they leaned away from the man. The vine tightened in a deadly squeeze around his throat.

They maintained their grip until the man's arms fell limply to his sides, and they were sure that he had died and that his strength and spirit had fled along the vine into their bodies.

With an exultant shout and wide smiles, they released the vine. The warrior's spirit would live on through them.

This experience was burned into Dick's mind. He would never forget it!

Chapter 5
Mysterious, Shining Guards

The chickens were the first to hear the unfamiliar footsteps creeping through the jungle, brushing past the undergrowth and hanging vines. The chickens squawked and fluttered into nearby huts on their bony legs, their claws scratching the dry earth. Hogs snorted into the dust and chased after them.

The men were out fighting. Only women and children remained behind. Ool had told Dick to stay home this time, too, much to the lad's disappointment. Frightened by the commotion, Lehtari bent down to peer out the door. Was their village also being attacked by a band of warriors? She called sharply to her children, and they came running. Within seconds, the village appeared empty. Even the animals were silent.

Just as silently, a visitor entered the village of Bartarmul and began setting up picture rolls in preparation for the lesson he would teach. Lehtari studied the visitor. A white man! Could he be a newcomer to the mission houses down on Malua Bay? Was this one of the men who owned the tall shining "angels"? Lehtari whispered the question to Dick, but he did not know.

Ool had whispered stories to her about going down to those houses to kill the missionaries and feast on them at the boiling hot springs rituals. "But the missionaries have guards around their houses," Ool had said, "big guards with flaming swords that they hold out to turn us back."

Ool had been amazed when he first saw them. Others had told him about the shining guards. Wanting to see them for himself, he had crept down the mountainside one morning and crouched behind the thick underbrush to observe the missionaries' small hut. But he saw no guards—only the missionary working in his garden.

That evening Ool was talking with a friend who had told him about the guards. "I did not see any guards around the white man's house," he said. "Are you sure you were not dreaming?"

"Ah, they are real all right," his friend replied. "But they only come out at night. You went during the daytime. Go at night, and you will see them!"

Not wanting to be thought a fool, and still very curious, Ool returned to the bay on the blackest night of the month, his dark skin blending into the darkness. He made his way stealthily down the hillside to the house of the missionaries.

Even as he neared the bay he could see a blue-white glow in the trees around the mission hut. His muscles tensed and he stooped low, peering through the dense undergrowth. Suddenly he gasped. Those were the tallest men he had ever seen! They surrounded the house shoulder to shoulder, leaving not a single unprotected place for an intruder to pass through. Their radiance was breathtaking. And the silence! Ool could almost hear the blood running through his veins.

Awed by what he had seen, Ool crept silently back into the forest and ran quietly toward home. He must warn his family—especially his bright and curious son, Dick. Ool was mystified by the power he had witnessed. With guards like that around the white men, it would be next to impossible to kill any of them! But though Ool marveled at their strength, he was also frightened. He didn't want the guards to become angry or come into his village for any reason. If they did come, he certainly would not be the one to turn them away!

Ool was also of a practical turn of mind. He wondered what he might do to enlist the protection of those shining guards for himself. Were the white man's guards the result of superior magic—a better connection to the world of the spirits?

Lehtari had wanted to see the angel guards, too, and wondered whether the missionary who came to the village that day had brought them along with him. She watched carefully as he set up his pictures under the trees. "I don't see the guards," she whispered to Dick as they studied the missionary cautiously.

"Of course you don't!" Dick reminded her. "Remember? The guards come out only at night. Father told us never to anger them, and if the missionaries ever come into our village, not to turn them away."

Lehtari nodded, wondering what to do. The white man was calling. Having spent four years in Australia, she understood what he said. He was calling the villagers to sit under the trees and learn about the pictures.

Dick studied the picture that the missionary was pointing to. It was a picture of a Man hanging on a wooden pole. Did the missionary want to warn the villagers what he would do to them if they did not come?

Lehtari listened carefully. "I want to tell you about this Man," the missionary said.

Lehtari stuck her head out the door. She saw other heads at the door of each hut in the village. The white man smiled. "Come," he said gently, motioning to the ground in front of the picture. "Come and sit down. I want to tell you about this Man. He cares about you."

Lehtari didn't know what to do. In their village, a woman was never to approach any man except her husband, and then only in privacy. If a group of men were talking, a woman must crawl past them no closer than thirty feet. She wondered what made the white man so different. How could he care about her when no one else did? And how did the Man on the wooden pole know her? She had never seen Him. With a sudden chill, she wondered if perhaps the shining guards had been spying on them without their knowledge. Perhaps she *should* find out about the man in the picture, if only to warn Ool. "Go on," she urged Dick, pushing him out the door. "Go find out about that man. We must tell your father so he can protect us."

"I won't go alone," Dick said, his dark eyes wide. "You have to come too!"

Lehtari's curiosity was intense. Remembering her lowly place in the caste system, she crawled slowly toward the missionary, stopping and squatting on the ground no closer than thirty feet from where he stood. Dick's two boy cousins and Ool's young new wife followed behind her.

When the other villagers saw Lehtari and her family approach the white man, their curiosity overcame them, too, and they joined the circle.

"Come! Sit down, sit down," the white man said again, nodding to the villagers. He held out his hands, palms up to show that he had no weapons to hide. He also held up his Bible.

"Ah, the black book that Nehambat said we must learn from," Lehtari thought.

The man introduced himself as Pastor W. D. Smith from Malua Bay. He told them that the Man in the picture was Jesus and that He had been killed because of His good works and because He was God's Son.

Lehtari was fascinated. She had thought the hogs were gods. Ool had worshiped them. But this Pastor Smith was telling her that there was *one* God who had *created* the hogs and everything else that was alive. Most important, Pastor Smith said that this God had sent His Son—His most cherished possession—to live on this earth so that *she* could know that God loved *her*.

Lehtari listened carefully. She must remember to tell Ool what the white man had said. If this God loved even the Little Nambus, then it was wrong of Ool to kill and eat them!

Even more incredible was the news that this God loved women! Lehtari had been told from the time she was a young girl that she counted for nothing more than to do a man's bidding. She thought she was of no value. But this Jesus had died for *her!*

After a while the missionary rolled up his pictures and said he was leaving. Lehtari wanted to beg him to stay, but she said nothing. But when the missionary promised to come again the next day for more stories, Lehtari's heart sang. All the rest of the day she and Dick discussed what they had heard. It was almost too incredible to believe.

Lehtari told her husband about the white man's visit. True to his word, Ool did not try to stop him from coming. He did not want to do anything that might stir up the anger of those guards! Besides, he might get the guards to protect him.

Pastor Smith came every day for several weeks. Soon Lehtari could not prepare the cannibal stew that Ool enjoyed. Slicing up human flesh had become distasteful to her. Jesus loved the very people that they cooked and ate!

One day Lehtari met Ool at the door of the hut.

"I'm hungry!" Ool said gruffly, pushing past her. "Why have you cooked only yams and nothing more?"

"I have been listening to the white man's stories," Lehtari said.

"You have been listening too much. You have no time left to complete your work," Ool said acidly.

"It does not take long to listen," Lehtari said. "That is not what stops me. I have enough time to cook for you. It is what the white man says that keeps me from doing the work that you expect of me."

"What do you mean?" Ool demanded, glancing around the room for something to threaten her with. Then, remembering his temper, he clenched his fists and held them to his sides.

"I'm giving you one chance to change the way you live," Lehtari said decisively. "You must stop eating human flesh. I will not cook it for you anymore. It is wrong."

Ool snorted and raised his fist menacingly. "What do you know of such things? And how dare you tell me that my family's ways are wrong?"

Lehtari held her ground. "If you do not change your ways, Ool, I will leave you and go live at Pastor Smith's place. I will also take Dick with me."

Ool spat on the ground. "If you go, I will drag you back," he boasted haughtily.

"And what of the shining guards?" Lehtari asked with a knowing smile. "If I am with Pastor Smith, they will protect me too."

Ool rubbed his chin thoughtfully and sat down with a resigned sigh to eat his meal of baked yams. He had to think this over.

During the next few days, while he considered Lehtari's threat, he stubbornly continued to bring human flesh home past the white man's home on Malua Bay. And just as stubbornly, Lehtari refused to cook it.

One day Ool returned home after a skirmish to find Lehtari gathering her few belongings and tying them together in sheets of bark. "What do you think you're doing?" he demanded.

"I'm leaving," Lehtari replied. She did not stop to talk, but continued gathering up her things and Dick's things. Her jaw was set firmly. "I'm not staying here where people worship pigs and kill and eat each other. This isn't the place for your son to grow up, either. You can do what you want, Ool, but I am not going to be a part of it, and neither is Dick. We're leaving!" There wasn't much to pack and she was finished almost as soon as she had begun.

Ool grabbed her arm as she started through the door, but she shook him away. "I am not afraid of you," she said. "I know that you are miserable. You hate yourself for what you did to Dick's mother and the other woman." Lehtari turned and looked at her husband with a kind expression on her face. "You are a good father, Ool. You can be an even better father if you will stop killing people and go with us to live near Pastor Smith. He can teach you many things."

"I don't know," Ool said, shaking his head. He looked into Dick's face and saw the pleading eyes of a twelve-year-old boy. "You believe what Pastor Smith says is true, don't you?" he said, tousling the dusty head of hair.

Dick nodded vigorously.

"You don't think it is a trick to get us to his village so he can use us as slaves?"

"Why does Pastor Smith need us as slaves?" Lehtari cut in. "He has his shining guards. They are strong enough to do any work he needs done."

Ool nodded thoughtfully.

Impatient, Lehtari lifted her bundles and moved toward the door.

"So you have really decided to leave," Ool said.

"Yes." Lehtari paused at the door. "And you?"

Ool considered her question. He had seen how the white people lived in Australia. It would not be too difficult to return to those ways. "You will not go alone," he said gruffly. "I will go with you." Then, in an attempt to regain his dignity as the head of the family, he pulled himself to his full height. "And I insist that my entire family go with me—both of my wives and my only son, Dick."

They built a new hut near Pastor Smith's home on Malua Bay. Mrs. Smith gave Lehtari and Ool's other wife two dresses each. It was the first time the women had ever covered their chests. There were other changes too. Gone were the pigs that used to smell up the place. Gone were the battles with warring tribes. Gone were the cannibalistic meals of human flesh. Gone was the spirit worship. In its place, Ool learned gardening from Pastor Smith, and he taught the pastor how to make thatched-roof buildings. Between what Ool taught the pastor and what the pastor knew about the building techniques used in Australia, they built a school where Ool learned carpentry. He and Pastor Smith spent many hours building desks and other furniture together.

Dick was impressed with the kind way that Pastor Smith treated his wife. In the villages, women were used as message carriers from one tribe to the other. Dick wondered, at first, if Pastor Smith was kind only to his wife. He was surprised to find that Pastor Smith treated *all* women with respect—even the native women! He began to think that if women had value as message carriers, maybe they *should* be treated with respect.

Two years later Ool died. Just before he died, he begged Pastor Smith, "Please don't take me back to Bartarmal when I die. Don't put my skull in the skull house. Leave me here. The mission will have Dick. I give him to you and to your God."

Dick remembered the day he saw a man die. He was thankful that his father did not have to endure a similar strangulation. More and more, he came to appreciate the gentleness he saw in the Smiths, and in their two sons, Ivan and Milton.

Though not enrolled as a student, Dick spent many hours with the boys as they worked in the garden and did their home study courses, asking questions and finding answers to many things that interested him. As he heard more and more Bible stories, Dick felt a strong desire to adopt a Christian name. He especially enjoyed the story of Samuel, who left his home as a young boy, much as he himself had done, to live with Eli the priest. Dick wanted to know more about the Christian God. This God had spoken to Samuel. Perhaps he spoke to all "Samuels." And so Dick became "Sam Dick."

Hearing of this, his mother, Lehtari, changed her name to "Ruth," and Ool's other wife changed her name to "Hannah." The trend caught on. Sam's two cousins, who lived with him and his mother, changed their names from Rosin and Melpikses to Shem and Philip.

Twenty-four years after Pastor Parker very nearly lost his life on Malekula, the missionaries had their first converts. It had been a slow, discouraging task, but the rewards were great!

Chapter 6

Mister One-Fifty-One

The morning was quiet on Malua Bay. The water sparkled, reflecting the clear blue sky, and quietly lapped the black volcanic sand. Overhead, an albatross glided silently, watching for the silver flash of a fish's tail in the water.

Sam Dick was busily hoeing in the garden with Milton, Pastor Smith's younger son and his very best friend. Though Sam was sixteen years old, he was barely four feet tall. Milton, very close to the same age, was much taller.

The earth was rich and sandy, turning easily under their tools. Sweating together under the sun, the boys worked without speaking for several minutes.

Sam heard the boat first. Leaning on his hoe, he stared out over the water, a hand over his eyes. "Who is that?" he asked.

Milton glanced at the small boat, then smiled when he saw the boat's name painted on its bow. "That's the *Loloma*,"[1] he said. "That's a mission boat."

Sam remembered when he and his family had gone to Australia on a much larger boat eleven years before. He had dreamed of sailing again and was hoping this boat might provide that opportunity. Unlike the plantation ship, this boat did not fire off cannons to get the islanders' attention.

"What are they here for?" Sam asked, remembering with a touch of concern the stories his father had told him about the slave ships that came in the past. "They are not here to kidnap us, are they?"

---

[1]In the Fijian language, "Loloma" means "love."

"Oh, no!" Milton chuckled. "The *Loloma* is not a slave ship. It's a missionary ship. I heard Father talking to Mother about it. They've been expecting it to come."

"But why are they coming?" Sam asked again.

"The church is building a new school on Aore," Milton explained. "The *Loloma* is here to invite the bigger boys to go with them to help clear the land, set out the plantation, and put up the building."

"Then the boys can't go to school?" Sam asked.

"Oh, they'll still go to school!" Milton exclaimed. "They'll work in the morning when it's cool and study in the afternoon in the shade."

"Will you go?" Sam asked.

Milton shook his head. "I guess not. I have to finish the lessons I've started. Besides, they want to take the big boys this time. There are a hundred and fifty boys from all the islands who want to go."

"Will they take me?" Sam wondered aloud.

"Doubt it. You're a bit too young—and too small."

Sam shrugged. He would have liked to see Aore again—the island where his family had worked the sugar plantations years before. He still carried warm memories of those days.

The students were abuzz that evening with excited chatter about the *Loloma*. Those who had been chosen to go busied themselves packing their things. They were leaving the next day. As Milton had said, Mr. Broad, the builder, had chosen only the oldest and strongest of the students.

Sam learned with a touch of envy that his cousin, Shem, had been chosen to go to Aore. The next day he went over to Shem and clapped him on the back. "So, you are one of the lucky ones!" he said with a nod.

Shem frowned. "I don't want to go," he said, staring at the floor. Self-consciously, he wiped a tear from his cheek, hoping nobody had seen.

"You're crying," Sam said. "What is wrong?"

"I'm frightened," Shem admitted. "I have never been off this island before in my life! I thought Philip was going, but Mr. Broad says he is too young. He can't go until next year. I don't know anyone else who is going."

"Mr. Broad told me I have to wait until next year too," Sam

said. "He thinks I will grow more if he gives me another year." He chuckled. "He doesn't know that my father was short too. Pastor Smith says I'll probably never be taller than my father."

Shem sniffed. "Have you told Mr. Broad that?"

"No—but maybe I should," Sam said thoughtfully. "Just maybe I should. Come with me. We'll talk to Mr. Broad together."

Mr. Broad came out of the Smiths' house with his usual smile. "Hello, Sam," he said, waving.

"Sir, hello!" Sam said, nodding his head. "Sir, I would like to talk to you about helping on the new school in Aore. I would like to go. Do you think I could go to school this year instead of next?"

"What's the hurry?" Mr. Broad asked. "You're going to grow, and, as I said, I'll be back for you next year."

"But my cousin is crying. Look at him." Sam nodded toward Shem. "He's lonely. No one from his village is going, so he has no friends. Couldn't I go with him? I'm only small, but inside these small arms is much strength. My father was small, too—and *he* was strong! I won't take up much room. . . . And I don't eat as much as those big boys. . . . And I can work!"

Mr. Broad smiled at Sam. He seemed so eager to go, and the Smiths had seemed impressed with his energy and enthusiasm. "Well, all right," he said shortly. "Get your things and come on board. We'll be sailing in an hour or two."

When Pastor Ross James, the other missionary on the "Loloma," heard about Sam, he called him "Mister 151," since he was the extra passenger on board the ship as it left Malekula Island for the Island of Aore to start a new school.

Chapter 7
Island Romance

Sam and the other boys followed Mr. Broad through the jungle as they staked out their claim for the school grounds. They pounded stakes into the earth and painted the letters "S-D-A" on them. Though the school would start small, they staked out enough land for growth and expansion.

Sam attended the Aore Missionary School for four years. He felt proud to be one of those who built it right out of the jungle! During those years at Aore he studied as hard as he worked, learning carpentry skills from Mr. Broad's example. He also watched the way Pastor James did his work as a teacher and principal, tucking his example away for future reference.

Because he had not started school when he was younger, Sam had a difficult time with his classes. He learned to count, add, and subtract. He could write, but with some difficulty. Put a newspaper in front of him, and he could only work his way through it with great difficulty. But give him the Bible, even a most unfamiliar passage, and he could read it fluently. He struggled with formal education, completing only the second grade.

But one thing came easily to Sam, and that was learning other languages. Though he could not write them, he found that he could speak the various island dialects within a few days of hearing them. At Aore, boys from many different islands came together to study, and Sam enjoyed learning their words for familiar objects and trying to talk with them. Within a week after he met someone whose language he did not know, he was able to carry on a conversation in his language. This gift was valuable, not only to the boys but also for the teachers, who enlisted Sam's interpretive skills when they could not communicate with the boys.

Sam left the school in 1931, when he was nineteen years old. So wonderful was his life as a Christian that he wanted to share what he had learned with heathen villages and bring them out of their fearful existence. But to his dismay, because he had only completed the second grade, he was not qualified to preach or to teach.

However, he was offered a job as a crewman on the mission boat *M. V. LePhare*. For several years he sailed between Aore and Espíritu Santo, and across to Malekula, his home island. He also sailed to the island of Ambrim, where Adventists now worked.

During a stopover in Aore in 1936, Sam was playing football with some of the students when someone touched his arm. It was Pastor Masing, a senior minister for that division. "I need to talk to you, Sam," he said with a smile.

Sam stepped off the playing field. "What do you want, Sir?"

"We've been meeting in committee. We need more teachers. Pastor Peacock, the mission president, has sent me to ask you to serve as a teacher at Baiap on the island of Ambrim."

Sam gasped. "Me?" he asked in astonishment. "I don't know enough to teach. Don't they that know I have only two grades of schooling?"

"Yes, we know that," Pastor Masing said, "but we believe you can do the job. The school at Baiap is a new one. Teach the people what you know, and then I guess they'll move you on to another place that needs you. Come and talk it over with Pastor Weil."

It was the break Sam had hoped for, but one that he had thought would always remain a dream. After talking with Pastor Weil and verifying that the job was actually his, Sam went to his room and knelt beside his bed. "Lord, I am not adequate to do what You ask," he whispered humbly. "You know that I have very little to teach the children. But You have a plan for me; I know that. My life has always been under Your eye." And then, remembering the symbolic ritual of the dying man and the vine, through which his strength and spirit was thought to have flowed, Sam prayed, "Lord, I have no vine to reach into Your presence so that Your Spirit may flow into me. But You throw down your vine to me, and I will hold it fast. I will be what You can make of me. My father fought for his people. I will be a warrior for You."

Sam left the next day on the ship to Ambrim with a small bundle of clothes and his Bible. With his outgoing personality and friendly smile, he made friends with everyone on the ship, but especially with Meshach and Norah, a married couple who were also setting out on a teaching assignment on the opposite side of the island of Ambrim. They had much in common and made plans, once they were settled, to get together as often as time permitted.

Sam's school at Baiap was only a year old. None of the students knew as much as Sam did, so even his limited education helped them. He had only seventeen students, but teaching them taxed his memory and his communication skills.

Using a picture roll much like the one he had first seen in his own village of Bartarmul, Sam told the students about Jesus and heaven and about how much better Christianity was than heathenism and animal worship.

But Sam didn't teach just Bible classes. He wanted to make learning fun and practical for his students. He started a Junior Missionary Volunteer program, including lessons in poison remedies, first aid, and tying knots, which he had learned as a crewman aboard ship. His students also learned the Junior Law and Pledge.

At the close of the first month of school Sam set out in his canoe for the village of Linbul, where Meshach and Norah were teaching, to take the tithes and offerings, as well as the school fees, to Pastor Weil. Paddling around the island and bucking the rolling swells alone took almost a full day. He felt relieved when at last he saw the school buildings in the distance.

The canoe scraped along the sand, and Sam hopped out, money bags in hand, to find Pastor Weil, who was passing through to collect the money. Norah was the first person he saw.

"Hello!" he said with a smile. "And how are you? Where's Meshach?"

Norah did not answer. She was obviously in distress, and as they walked toward the school, she told Sam that her husband was dead.

"But why? How?" Sam asked, remembering how he felt when his father died.

Norah explained that they had begun their teaching well, with no reason to suspect that the villagers were disturbed. As was the custom, the villagers raised pigs and worshiped them. The pigs were a nuisance in Meshach's garden, digging up the seeds and disturbing the new growth, but Meshach had not hit or thrown sticks at the pigs—he had done the next best thing. He built a fence around his garden to keep out the pigs.

The villagers mistrusted anyone who did not share their esteem of pigs, so they had poisoned Meshach. He died a month after he started teaching at the school.

Seeing how upset Norah was, Sam didn't think it was right to leave her alone on the island with hostile people, so he stayed a couple of days longer than he had originally intended. However, he didn't think it was proper to ask her to return to Baiap with him.

Norah, however, had ideas of her own. One evening she asked Pastor Weil to visit in her home. After Pastor Weil had settled himself in his chair, Norah came straight to the point. "Meshach and I dedicated our lives to working for the church," she said. "Now he is dead. I want to follow this man, Sam Dick."

"What do you mean, Norah—'follow him' ? "

"He has no one to care for him," Norah explained. "I have no one to care for. I'll go with him to Baiap and look after him."

Pastor Weil was surprised. "That wouldn't be right, Norah. It wouldn't look good for a pastor to have a woman living in his home if he was not married to her! I can't let you do that."

"I'm going to follow him," Norah persisted.

"Then you must marry him."

"Will you speak to Sam for me?" Norah asked.

Pastor Weil agreed.

It was a new idea to Sam. He hadn't thought about marriage, and much less had he thought about marrying Norah! She was his friend's wife. But as he thought about it, it seemed like a good idea. Norah had been at the school for a little while. She knew what teaching was all about. She had shown courage, and she was even shorter than he was! It didn't take him long to make up his mind. "I will marry Norah," Sam told Pastor Weil.

They were married that afternoon under the coconut palms with the vast ocean and volcanic islands as a backdrop, and Pastor Weil their witness and minister. The next morning they left for Sam's school in Baiap. It was easier this time. Norah helped with the paddling. Sam could see, already, how much she would help his work.

Chapter 8
Prisoners!

When war broke out in Europe, most of the Australian and New Zealand missionaries left the islands in haste to return to their countries. Sam and Norah, and other native teachers like them, were left behind to carry on as best as they could.

Four years after they were married, Sam and Norah and their son Jonathan left the school at Baiap and moved to an island called Paama. Just twenty-five miles in circumference, and with especially rich soil, Paama was the most populated of the islands. Its people were considered wealthy by local standards because of the trading they did with merchant ships. Their sandalwood, coffee, cocoa, and cotton were prized items, as well as the dried coconut meat, called copra.

But the people of Paama resented Christians. "The white man's religion," they called it. Not knowing enough about the missionaries, and lumping them in the same category as the white slave traders who had terrorized the islands years before, they were suspicious of everything that Sam and Norah did. They wanted them off their island—at any price! With the white missionaries gone, the natives decided to "settle the score."

Ulas, one of the chief men of the village of Tevale, where Sam and Norah lived, stirred up the people. He suggested that they make Sam and Norah so miserable and so frightened that they would leave.

One day Sam and Norah found that a cooking pot was missing. Vegetables vanished from their garden. On Sabbath morning, as Sam and Norah tried to worship with a handful of believers, they heard a pig squeal. Going outside, they found it slaughtered in their yard, its blood spurted everywhere.

However, Sam and Norah were not intimidated, so Ulas decided to take firmer action. "If we take the teachers away from their school," he told the villagers, "the school will die."

Sam and Norah had just finished their worship the next morning when Ulas led his men into their yard. They were shouting and banging wooden shields together.

"Where's the Adventist teacher? Bring him out!" they yelled.

Sam reminded Norah of the vine and of God's strength and spirit entering into them through prayer. He didn't run or panic. If God had a plan, surely this would fit into it.

"I'm here," Sam called, stepping out of his neatly kept hut. "What do you want?"

"We've come to finish the work of the Adventists. We're taking you away!" Ulas declared.

"You have no power to end God's work," Sam replied. "You can take me away, but His work will go on."

"We'll see about that. Get your wife and children. Pack up all your belongings and come with us."

In the face of spears and clubs, Sam could only obey. He didn't know that a few miles away, in the village at Loulep, their friends Isaac and Sarah were going through the same thing.

Norah and Sam packed their belongings as quickly as they could. They didn't have very much—one change of clothes apiece, a book or two, a few pots and pans. Fearing the worst, Sam also gathered his chalk and exercise books and his beloved picture rolls.

"Hurry, or we'll kill you!" Ulas shouted.

The noise of the pack brought people out of their huts. On one side, a large number of supporters gathered behind the angry chief. On the other side stood Sam and his school children with a few of the braver parents. Ulas was a "big man"—a leader—and the people feared him.

Sam tried to comfort his friends. "We'll go with them," he said. "But don't you worry. God's work won't die. These men have tried to burn down the church at Loulep. Now they're trying to burn down God's work here. They can strike all the matches of persecution they want to. They can pour on all the anger and hate they can find, but they cannot burn down what God is building."

Sam remembered the stories in Revelation about Satan's

trying to attack God's church, making war with God's remnant. How would it all fit together in God's plan?

Sam began to tie up the door and the window screens. "You needn't do that," one of his tormentors called. "You won't be back!"

Sam drew himself up to his full height of four feet and looked directly into the leader's eyes. "You cannot stop God's work," he said confidently. "We will return." Just how, he didn't know, because his attackers had the upper hand.

As they trudged along the coast of Paama, Sam whispered to Norah. "What do you think? Will they harm us?"

Her tiny form straightened. "No. They might try, but God will take care of us. I know He has much more for you to do. This isn't the end for us."

After two hours, they entered the coastal village of Tavie, where Adventist missions had not yet arrived. To their astonishment, they saw Isaac and Sarah with their children under guard at the base of two coconut palms.

Ulas jabbed at them. "Over there. Join your friends. And listen well to the *Jonga Nemelo'un* [talking chief]. You and your work are finished."

A chief appeared, his spokesman behind him. Sam was not intimidated. His father, Ool, had been the talking chief in his own village of Bartarmul. Had Sam stayed in his village, *he* would now be the talking chief of Bartarmul.

The spokesman explained the situation to the group of curious villagers. "The chief and the elders have decided that the Seventh-day Adventist mission must stop its work on Paama," he said. "We have taken their two teachers and their families from Loulep and Tevale and brought them here to Tavie because they have no friends to help them here.

"Our decree is that no one shall bring them food or water. We will test their God. They believe He is powerful and will help them. We know better. He will not come to deliver them.

"Be warned. Anyone who helps these Adventists will suffer for it. We are setting guards to see that they don't escape and that no one comes to help them."

The crowd murmured, and then, at the command of the chief, they straggled off to their huts.

The two families were placed under guard inside a fenced

enclosure. Their only shelter was a single coconut palm whose fronds waved in the tropical breeze.

The first night went reasonably well. It is not cold on Paama, and the lack of shelter didn't trouble the two families too much. As soon as daylight came, Sam suggested that they have worship together. The families held hands as first Isaac and then Sam prayed. For a moment Sam remembered holding the vine around that old man's throat at Bartarmul. How different this was! They were holding hands with God, and He was going to help them. As a true warrior of the Lord, he stiffened his resolve. He would not yield.

Sam brought out his picture rolls, and soon a small crowd had gathered. The people were enthralled with the pictures, but the guards held them back.

Sam chose to tell the story of Shadrach, Meshach, and Abednego. Without actually talking to the villagers, he told the story loudly enough that they could hear. They listened intently. "That's what we're like," Sam said. "God's enemies have put us into a furnace of trial. They have laughed at God and said that He can't deliver us. But I know He will.

"Do you know why they put these three men in the flames?" Sam asked. "Because they would not yield to the heathen king of Babylon. God set them free so they could worship Him. When they were free, even the king bowed down to God." He turned to the group of villagers. "You have us as prisoners now, but let me ask you this: When God sets us free, will you promise to worship Him as we do?"

Heads nodded. Sam wondered when it would happen.

That evening Sam's gaze followed the rough trunk of the coconut tree above them. A cluster of coconuts hung directly overhead. "I'm going to climb that tree and throw down some coconuts for the children to eat," he said. He managed to twist off two or three. The coconut milk satisfied the thirsty children, and the sweet white coconut meat took away a little of their hunger.

After the villagers had eaten their evening meals, they again gathered around the prisoners, curious to see what would happen. Sam spoke directly to the crowd. "Many of you call yourselves Christians," he said, "but you haven't treated us as Christians should. Jesus said you should bring food and water to those in prison. We're in your prison, and you haven't helped us."

Some in the crowd began to murmur in sympathy. Later, during the dark hours when the guards were asleep, someone slipped them a little water and baked cassava.

By the third day of their capture, Sam and Isaac were desperate. The coconuts easiest to reach had long since been taken down and consumed, and the children were suffering. But Sam told his little group, "God delivered Jonah after three days. Today I believe we shall be freed."

Back in Tevale, Ulas had a visitor. The British district officer, Captain Adams, came stalking into the village with his official entourage. Captain Adams was a big man—over six feet tall, with fiery red hair and a booming voice to match. "Where's the Adventist teacher?" he asked.

No one offered an answer.

"Come on, don't play games. What have you done with him? Boiled and eaten him?" Captain Adams laughed at his crude joke.

Still no answer. Immediately the captain became suspicious. He went about his business, inspecting houses and sanitation, offering suggestions on gardening and hygiene, checking for malaria and other common illnesses. Finally someone sidled up to him.

"They've taken Sam Dick and his family to Tavie and put them in prison there."

"In prison! Whatever for?"

"Ulas stirred up the people to get rid of the Adventists. A gang of men came and dragged them off."

Captain Adams set out immediately for Tavie. The noise of his arrival brought the whole village out. Captain Adams didn't pause at the edge of the village as he usually did, but strode into its center. "Where have you got the prisoners?" he called out. "Take me to them."

But he had already seen the little group under the coconut palm. He could see their distress. His men brushed aside the guards and brought water to the thirsty families.

By this time Ulas and his co-conspirators had come on the scene.

Captain Adams turned to Ulas, and his eyes narrowed. "What's going on here? What crime have these men committed? Why have you refused them food and water? Do you plan to kill them?"

The men pushed Ulas forward. After all, this was *his* idea. Ulas was uncharacteristically ill at ease. His voice lacked its usual power as he began. "We didn't want the Adventists here in the first place. They teach our people not to eat pigs. They keep a different day of worship. They won't let us have more than one wife. They're a nuisance. We want them out!"

Captain Adams cut him short. "How long have they been here?"

"Seven years," came the sullen reply.

"Seven years! They've been here seven years, and *now* you decide you don't want them? Ridiculous! Now you all listen to *me*! Let them free at once. Take all their belongings back to their villages and place them in order in their houses. Do not break one thing, and do not steal one thing. If anything is missing or broken, you will be the ones in jail. And it won't be under a coconut palm, either. It will be the calaboose in Vila for you!"

A few hours later the families parted and went to their homes, accompanied by policemen from the district officer's party. Never again would they have trouble like this on Paama.

Sam and Norah had their praise session. Sam's prayer vine still reached up to God, and He was sending His angels to see that nothing would hinder His plan.

Chapter 9

Under the Wings of an Angel

With the missionaries gone, the local pastors had many concerns. For some of them, the salary of two dollars per month did not go far enough. Sam often had to sell vegetables from his garden or go fishing to keep Norah and the children alive.

When Japan bombed Pearl Harbor in December of 1941, the islands of the South Pacific became important to both the Japanese and the American armies, though they were against each other.

One morning a policeman arrived in Paama and announced that everyone in the village must come to an important meeting that night. Sam attended the meeting with a knot in his stomach. What kind of news would he hear?

"I have a message from the District Officer," the policeman said. "World War II is on. All pastors, teachers, and chiefs must assemble at Leero this Monday. Captain Adams will be there to talk to you."

He explained that each village would be required to provide young men to go to Port Vila. "The Americans want a bigger place to land their planes," he said. "Those planes you see flying over Paama are only little ones. They want to bring in big planes. We must widen and extend the landing strip so that bigger planes can land."

He told everyone to appear in Leero in one week. "We will have a ship to transport you to Port Vila. This is an order. No one will be let off. If you try to hide or run away, we will send the police to find you. Then you will still have to go to Vila, but you will live in the jail and will get no pay."

To Sam it all sounded like the old days when white men kidnapped the islanders for slave labor. Homes were broken up, and some of the young men never came back. Furthermore, if the fighting came to Vila, his people would die alongside the Americans and the Japanese.

Sam walked away from the meeting with his head bowed, thinking and praying as he trudged back home. "What will it mean for my church members?" he wondered. "So many of them are new in their faith. Dear God, You care for my people. You have brought the Sabbath message to them. Teach me how to help them stay true to You."

Sam was certain that if he went to Vila, he and the others would be forced to work on Sabbath. He mustn't let his people go to Vila unless he had a promise that they wouldn't have to work on Sabbath. With that resolve, he turned back toward town and walked into the government office building. More than a little fearful, he knocked on the partially open door to Captain Adams' office.

"Yes, yes," the British soldier said impatiently, "what do you want?"

Sam stepped inside. "Sir, I am Sam Dick," he said respectfully. "Do you remember the man whom you set free from prison in Tavie? I'm the Seventh-day Adventist teacher from Loulep."

"Yes, I remember. What is it then?"

"It's about this airfield. You will pay our people, of course."

"That's a matter for the Americans, but yes, I'm sure you will be paid, and paid well. Why do you ask?"

"I'm asking you to pay my people and me less than the others."

Captain Adams' attention was arrested. This was Paama, money capital of the New Hebrides! "Less? What do you mean, less?" his voice boomed. The natives really had no interest in this war. They usually took all they could get. It couldn't be patriotism or a voluntary contribution to the war effort that motivated this preacher! He was intrigued. "Go on," he said.

"We're Sabbath keepers, Sir. We don't work on Sabbath, the seventh day of the week. We won't be working on Saturday because it is our day of worship."

Captain Adams' ruddy face became red like iron in a fire. "Not work?" he exploded. "Nonsense! You'll do as you're told!" He stood up and towered nearly two feet above the little teacher.

"This is a war! You have no choice. You will work when we say."

Sam shook his head. "You don't understand. We cannot break God's command. We won't work. Even if you put us in jail, we won't work."

"We'll see about that," the captain threatened. "I'm a Catholic. I'd like to take Sunday off, but I have to work. Bring your men on Monday. They must come and work the same as all the rest."

Captain Adams sat down, and Sam was dismissed.

Back in Loulep, Sam called the Adventists together and told them what had happened. "I'm not going to Vila," he said. "If you go, you must stay true to the Sabbath. They'll come for me next week, but I won't be going."

So Sam didn't make the trip the next Monday. He knew that Captain Adams would have his name on a list and that the police would come looking for him when his name was circled as missing.

Norah and the children went off to hide in the forest while Sam stayed hidden near their house. All Monday night he watched for the police to arrive, ready to flee into the bush when they did. They never came.

By Tuesday morning Sam was desperately tired. "They will not come for me now," he reasoned, and he slipped into his hut, leaving the door open so he could hear the police if they came. Then he slept.

Toward the end of the day, Sam awoke. The house was dark. And what was that sound? Somebody crying? It was Norah! Outside! "Norah!" he called. "What's the matter? Why are you crying? Are the police coming?"

"Sam? . . . Sam!" Norah burst into the hut. "You're here! They didn't take you away! Where did you hide? How come they didn't find you?"

"Hide?" Sam asked. "I haven't been out of this house. I've been here all the time, asleep."

"But the police came looking for you. They looked in all the huts. I saw them look through the door of this hut. You *must* have hidden, or they would have seen you!"

"I didn't hide anywhere," Sam said again. "They just didn't see me. God must have put His hand over me, or over their eyes, I don't know which." He smiled broadly. "It's a miracle, Norah. God performed a miracle for us today!"

Realizing that his family was unsafe on the island of Paama,

Sam decided to take them to live with Pastor Masing on Ambrim. They would leave under cover of darkness. The journey itself was risky, paddling a canoe over the rolling seas in the dark, but it seemed to Sam the least dangerous of their choices.

A terrible rain blew in that night, shortly before they were to leave. Sam watched the downpour with concern. They *had* to leave tonight, rain or not. After the village women had called their children in, he called to Norah and they hurried away from their hut, young Jonathan in Sam's arms, their belongings held above their heads as protection from the rain. Their canoe was tied up in the lagoon. They stuffed their few belongings inside the narrow opening, and then found a place for Jonathan. There was no room in the canoe for even a small adult to squeeze in. Norah and Sam would have to keep their balance on planks tied across the canoe, their legs crammed into the narrow opening.

A strong gust of wind blew the palm trees on the beach, sending a dead branch crashing to the sand. Sam tried to listen to the rhythm of the waves. A narrow sliver of moonlight glistened on the water beyond the reef. Sam pushed the canoe into the waves, jumped on, and paddled furiously. At that very moment, a huge wave sucked the canoe away from the shore. Sam paddled into the next breaker, and the next. Finally, the canoe broke through the crashing surf to the calmer waters of the deep ocean beyond.

Sam paddled continuously for the next two hours while Norah bailed. They were exhausted by the time they neared the coast of Ambrim Island.

Sam knew that Ambrim was surrounded by a coral reef with just one entrance. He listened for the roar of the surf on the reef, hoping to follow the sound to the entrance to the lagoon. He strained his ears, but heard nothing. Suddenly the canoe scraped on the bottom. The reef? Surely not! He would have heard the breakers. He put his hand over the side of the boat and gingerly felt the water. Then he reached into it and felt sand. The beach! Without even realizing it, they had sailed through the entrance and found the beach! With such a Pilot, why should they ever fear Captain Adams and his army?

Pulling the boat up onto the sandy beach, the family settled down to wait for morning. Sam knew this place. It would take a full day or more to walk to the mission at Linbul. But before long Jonathan was crying for food. With skills learned from childhood, Sam headed off toward the forest, looking for the telltale vines that showed the presence of wild yams. Some of these yams weighed as much as seventy or eighty pounds each! One was enough to feed a whole family!

Sam kept one eye on the ground, the other in the trees above, watching for snakes that might drop down on him. It was obvious that no one had been through here for some time. Before long, Sam spotted a withering vine. He dug in the ground and unearthed two fine yams, smaller than he had hoped to find, but enough to feed a whole family.

Back at the beach, he searched for driftwood, hoping to find two pieces that would be dry enough to burn. The rain had soaked everything. For over an hour Sam rubbed various sticks and stones together, but he could not strike a fire. Not even a spark appeared.

"Shouldn't we pray?" Norah suggested.

Sam had not forgotten his prayer vine. He just hadn't thought to cling to it. They prayed a simple prayer, asking God to help Sam make a fire. Opening his eyes, Sam picked up two pieces of wood lying just where they had prayed. They looked no different from any of the others he had tried. He took a deep breath, willing himself to believe in God's power. Then he placed the smaller piece of wood into a groove in the other piece. All his senses were focused on those two sticks. A moment later the larger piece was smoking. Carefully he blew on it and placed shreds of dry wood chips and leaves around the smoking hole. The smoke turned into a tiny red glow. A few more puffs and the leaves and chips caught fire and flamed brightly. Five minutes later the fire was blazing. An hour later they enjoyed delicious roasted yams.

Their energy renewed, Sam and Norah began the long walk to the mission station on the other side of the island, where they rested for three weeks. Then Sam learned that Captain Adams was returning to check on the work the natives were supposed to be doing. Sam decided to go back and face the captain. It might mean jail or a forced trip to Vila, but Sam wasn't worried. He felt the need to make sure that Captain Adams knew he had not broken the Sabbath as the captain had said he would.

Sam stood once more at the door to Captain Adams' office and knocked. "Yes, yes, come in," Captain Adams called. He sounded annoyed.

"Hello, Sir!" Sam smiled his usual broad smile. "Do you remember Sam Dick, the Adventist teacher who came and talked to you last time you were here?"

"Yes, yes. Of course I remember. He was a lazy man. He wanted to take a holiday when everyone else was working."

"Did you find him when you went looking for him?"

Captain Adams shuffled the papers on his desk. "We found everyone we went looking for," he said, avoiding a direct response.

The little teacher shook his head. "No, you didn't. I'm Sam Dick. You didn't find me!"

Now the captain shook *his* head. "No, you're not Sam Dick! I'd know that fellow anywhere! After all, I set him free at Tavie, didn't I? You're not the man."

"Yes, I am."

"No, you're not."

"Truly, Sir, I am the man."

They argued for quite a while, Sam telling him how the police came looking but couldn't find him, the captain insisting that they had a full list of recruits and that Sam was someone else.

Finally, Captain Adams leaned back in his swivel chair and sighed. "You're a Christian teacher, aren't you?"

"Yes, Sir," Sam replied, nodding his head.

"Well, you're the only Christian teacher left on Paama. The others have all gone to Vila—Presbyterians, Catholics, Adventists—they've all gone."

Sam knew it was true.

"I tell you what," Captain Adams continued, "I'll make you pastor of all Paama—the pastor of all the churches of all the faiths on the entire island! If God has kept you out of my clutches, He must have something special for you to do. Now you must be everybody's pastor. I'll tell the police and the chiefs. They will watch out for you and give you safe passage wherever you go."

And so it was that Sam became "Pastor Sam" of the entire wealthy island of Paama, appointed not by the church, but by a government officer!

Chapter 10
Unwilling Thief

Sam enjoyed pastoring on the island of Paama and was often seen in his traditional ministerial clothes—black shorts and white shirt—visiting the sick and offering comfort to the bereaved. In his sermons he preached about the Sabbath and shared his faith with Catholics, Presbyterians, and those simply curious about religion in general.

One day Sam stared across the strait between Paama and the smaller island of Lopevi. In the distance its volcano was smoking, as usual. For the first time he thought about taking Christianity to that island. There were no Adventists on Lopevi, and he wanted to share the good news with those people too.

With the help of a friend, Sam spent one whole day paddling to Lopevi. He visited several houses and invited the people to attend a meeting in the evening, where he promised to show special pictures and tell stories. Several came. One man in particular, John Fred—known as "the big man teacher" from another island—came to ask Sam a burning question: "Why do you keep the seventh day as the Sabbath?"

Sam simply opened his Bible and showed Mr. Fred what it said. "Every Christian has only one mirror in which to see himself," Sam said. "That mirror is the Bible. If you look into that mirror, Jesus will show you what to do."

Mr. Fred didn't argue. He just listened. The villagers standing around also listened interestedly.

Mr. Fred went home.

Several months later Sam received a message to come to John Fred's village and baptize him. He had "looked into the mirror" and had seen that he must keep the Sabbath. He declared his island an Adventist island and began preaching to everyone there.

Sam was delighted, and even more encouraged to spread the word to other islands where no Adventists had ever gone before.

In 1944, Sam was appointed pastor of the larger island of Tanna. On his way to Tanna, he visited Port Vila, where Captain Adams had had his office many years before. Now there were many Adventist soldiers and sailors there, and they were delightful to visit with. But there were also soldiers and sailors on the island who had nothing but bad intentions on their minds.

Walking through Port Vila one evening, an army jeep stopped beside Sam.

"Come, help us!" a voice called out.

Sam looked into the face of a young American soldier. The soldier seemed friendly. "What do you want me to do?" Sam asked, returning the smile.

"I've got some things I want moved from one place to another. I'll give you forty dollars if you stick with me until I've finished."

Forty dollars! That was an immense sum of money to someone whose monthly wage was about four dollars. Sam climbed into the jeep, glad to help, and glad to be paid so much for helping.

They went first to an army store where they loaded all kinds of goods into the jeep. Then they headed off to the other side of town.

Sam helped unload the goods, wondering why they were leaving them here, at the edge of the forest. Suddenly he realized that he was helping the soldier steal from the army store. Natives came out of the forest quietly, paid the soldier, and began carting the goods away.

Sam felt sick. "Excuse me," he said to the soldier. "I'm a Christian. I cannot let you steal like this. It's not right. Please stop. Let me help you take the goods back to the store."

The soldier guffawed. "A Christian, eh? S'pose you're looking for Heaven! After the war, come to America. America is a second heaven."

"Please," Sam persisted. "Please don't do this. I'll help you take it all back. You don't even need to pay me! I won't take money earned by stealing." He walked off alone, toward the city.

"Don't you want your money?" the soldier shouted after him. "You're a fool!"

Sam Dick knew he would have been a fool to keep the money. He wondered if what the soldier said about America was true. If America really was as good as heaven, would he ever get a chance to see it for himself?

Chapter 11
Dead or Alive?

Norah and Sam's second son, James, was burning up with a fever. The situation was similar to the one Sam Dick's mother had faced years before. Tanna was still fairly backwards by Western standards. Because of World War II, no buses ran on the island. Nobody had cars. The most fortunate owned horses.

Sam and Norah still had few possessions, and certainly not a car or a horse. They had to go everywhere on foot or by boat. The nearest doctor was more than thirty miles away, on the other side of the island, and Sam was out teaching in one of the villages.

Norah worried over James, pressing damp cloths on his forehead to cool him down. He was so quiet and still. What should she do? Unlike Sam's mother, Norah was not entirely helpless. Her husband would allow her to go for help. But help was thirty miles away on the other side of the island!

Desperate, Norah decided to walk across the island with her son in her arms to visit the Presbyterian doctor. Jonathan, their older son, would have to go along with them. His little legs kept up a steady pace as he followed along the dirt road beside his mother.

Norah perspired heavily in the humid jungle heat. James's little shirt clung to his chest, and his feverish head on her shoulder made Norah even hotter than she would normally have been. They walked for most of the day. At last, near exhaustion, and with burning feet, Norah gratefully placed her young son on the hospital bed under the care of the doctor and collapsed in a chair beside him.

The doctor gave James some medicine, and he improved

within one hour. Then the doctor told Norah that she could take her son home, and he gave her directions on how to give James more medicine.

On weary feet, Norah started slowly for home, carrying James in her aching arms. It was more difficult now, though. The child twisted in her arms to look at the things they were passing, and sometimes he reached out and touched Jonathan's head as he walked beside them.

A horse and rider appeared ahead—a common enough sight on this trail. Just what happened next, Norah would never know, but as the horse passed her, it suddenly bucked and kicked. One hoof caught Jonathan on the chest, throwing him across the path into the grass several feet away.

Norah screamed. She laid the baby down and hurried to Jonathan's side. He wasn't breathing, and she was sure that he was dead.

Just as Norah bent over the small, still form, wondering what to do, Sam arrived. Knowing that James was sick, he had finished teaching early and gone home. Norah was not there when he arrived, and, guessing that she had taken James to the doctor, he walked and jogged across the island to meet her.

Unaware of the accident that had just occurred, Sam brushed past the horrified rider on his horse and hurried over to Norah, calling her name.

"Jonathan is dead!" Norah screamed, holding her head in her hands.

"What happened?"

"That horse kicked him. Look! You can see the hoof mark on his chest."

Sure enough, a perfect hoof print reddened the boy's skin just above his heart. Sam put his ear to the boy's chest. Nothing. He held a piece of grass to his mouth and nose. No breath. Norah must be right. The horse must have killed his boy. Normally quiet and dignified, Sam was not himself when faced with this shock. He scrambled to his feet and started toward the horseback rider.

"You killed my son!" he shouted at the lad on the horse, and he broke into sobs. "He's dead! My son is dead!"

The young man took one look and galloped off. Back in his village, he flung himself off his horse, wailing, "My horse has killed a boy! My horse has killed a boy!"

He ran into his hut and came out brandishing a knife. "The police will come and get me. I've killed a boy!"

Hearing the commotion, the village chief came out. The young man wept and told his story once more. "I'm going to kill myself, but first I must kill the horse." He moved toward the nervous, side-stepping animal, his knife ready.

"Stop!" the chief ordered.

Tears streaming down his face, the lad stopped, still staring at the horse.

"Did you tell the horse to kick the boy?" the chief asked.

The boy shook his head. "No, but they'll want revenge. They'll come and want my life for his. I might as well die now as later."

"If you didn't mean to kill the boy, don't blame yourself," the chief said. "We'll sort it out."

With great difficulty the chief persuaded the boy to put the knife away. "You stay in my hut," he said.

Meanwhile, Sam scooped up his son and ran back blindly along the trail toward the doctor's house. Norah followed, with James in her arms. How fortunate that she had just left the hospital when the horse came by!

In moments the doctor had his stethoscope over the boy's heart. "The boy is not dead," he said. "I can hear his heart."

"But he *was* dead!" Sam declared. "I couldn't hear his heart or feel his pulse. He wasn't breathing!"

"Here, listen for yourself," the doctor said, handing the stethoscope to the pastor.

A few minutes later Jonathan stirred, sat up, and felt his chest. "It hurts here, Daddy," he said. "What happened?" Then looking around the hospital, he said, "I'm not sick—Jimmy is! What am I doing here?"

With a relieved smile and kisses and hugs, Norah told Jonathan what had happened.

"We must find the boy on the horse and show him that you are all right," Sam said. "I'm afraid I frightened him, though I didn't mean to."

"Then we can go home?" Jonathan asked.

"You're fine," the doctor assured him. "You're going to be just fine!"

Norah and Sam carried their sons into the village, asking for the boy on the horse. As they suspected, everyone in the village knew what had happened, and everyone was afraid that they had come for revenge. Nobody would tell them where the boy lived.

At last they found the chief. When he learned that Sam and Norah had come to show the boy that their son was all right, he called the boy from the back of his hut. A smile broke over the boy's face as he saw Jonathan standing in front of him, alive and well in spite of the red hoof print still on his chest.

"It's a miracle," Sam told the boy. "It is because of the power of the God in heaven that our boy is again alive."

Chapter 12
Mysterious Visitor

Sam Dick was ordained as a minister in 1951, fifteen years after he began working for the church. He now spoke seven or eight New Hebridean languages and was an active adviser to the mission executive committee. Because he still could not read very well, he had to depend on his memory for his sermons and sermon notes. This was not uncommon for his people. Theirs is an "oral society," which passes along stories and culture by word of mouth rather than by the written page. As a result, their memorization skills are very sharp.

While Sam was at Aore School for the ordination service, Pastor Hiscox, the principal, told him that he had visited Mavea Island recently. "I found a friend of the church there who wants us to come and start a school, Sam. This is just what we need. When considering whom I should send, I immediately thought of you."

Sam listened quietly.

The principal continued. "You have a kind spirit, Sam. We have no work on Mavea, and we feel that you will do a good job there."

"Can I take Norah with me?" Sam asked. They had four children by now, and he hated leaving her and the children alone for extended periods of time.

"It might be easier if you went alone," Pastor Hiscox suggested. "You won't be gone long for this first visit, and Norah and the children can come later, after you've found a place for them to stay."

"Let me take Jonathan," Sam pleaded. "At least he's company, and he's old enough to help out in many ways."

"OK," Pastor Hiscox agreed.

On the day they left Tanna, Sam had just a few belongings with him: a bush knife, an ax, one change of clothing, and some uncooked rice. They also took along a fishing net, just in case they should need to provide their own food.

Arriving at their destination, Pastor Hiscox brought the little mission ship in as close to the shore as possible. Because of the dangerous, spiky coral that could tear a hole in the bottom of the ship, they took a flat-bottomed dinghy from the ship to the shore. Luckily, the tide was in, and the water was high enough that the dinghy floated safely over the needle-sharp coral spikes. Pastor Hiscox helped Sam and Jonathan unload their things on the beach. The only shelter was a thatched-roof shed with no walls—little protection from the sun, and practically no protection from the rains, should they come.

There was no sign of anyone waiting for them.

Sam looked up and down the beach. "Where is your friend?" he asked Pastor Hiscox. "Isn't he to meet us here?"

"This is the place he said he'd meet you today. I have to get back to the mission station, so I can't stay, but I'm sure he'll be here soon." With a hasty wave, Pastor Hiscox climbed back into the dinghy and rowed back to the ship. It putt-putted away, and within a few minutes was out of sight around the beachhead.

All day Sam and Jonathan scanned the coral beach in both directions. Jonathan investigated the fringes of the jungle, but saw no one. Finally the sun began to sink on the horizon, throwing beautiful rainbow colors across the sky.

Knowing that in minutes it would be dark, Sam lighted a small fire. He pulled out a cooking pot, filled it with briny salt water, and poured in some rice. Squatting beside the fire, he began idly stirring the pot, wondering what they should do for the night. Fortunately, Jonathan was not worried. He was wading in the shallows with the net, trying to catch some fish. All at once he shouted, "Look, Daddy! Someone's coming."

Sam stopped stirring the rice. Sure enough, someone was on a point of land not far away. But Sam realized with dismay that it was a young boy, and he wasn't coming toward them. He was fishing too!

"Shall I go and talk with him?" Jonathan asked.

"No, I don't think so. He's only a boy. We might frighten him.

Let's wait and see what happens. Besides, you don't know his language."

The stranger flicked his fishing line in their direction and walked toward them. They could tell that he was both curious and afraid. He gradually came closer, till he was close enough to talk.

Sam looked up from the rice and smiled, but he didn't say anything.

Finally the boy decided that a boy and a smiling little man cooking rice weren't much of a threat, and he tried to tell them something. However, Sam had guessed right: They did not speak the same language. The boy sat silently then, watching the fire while the rice cooked. Presently, he laid two little fish on the coals. When the fish were cooked, he gave one to Jonathan, in the custom of his people, and accepted rice from them in exchange.

Jonathan and the boy played together in the water until it was time to go to sleep. Then they all curled up around the fire and settled in for the night.

The next morning, while the boy took Jonathan fishing, Sam was approached by two strangers—a local man and a woman. To Sam's surprise, they knew one of the dialects which he also knew, and they could communicate with each other. They told Sam that they had been searching for their son all night long. Finally they had thought of looking here, at his favorite fishing place. Had Sam seen the boy?

Sam told them he had fed the boy supper. "He's over there now with my son," he said, pointing to the silhouettes of Jonathan and the boy fishing on the point. The boy's mother was obviously relieved. To show her thanks, she offered to cook a meal for everyone right there under the thatched roof. By then it was too late to start for the village, so that night all five of them curled up around the fire to sleep.

The next morning the boy's father, Raht, asked Sam if he wanted them to help him build a house. When Sam nodded, the man started clearing the land with his bush knife. Sam helped, but because the jungle was so thick there, progress was slow. The boy's father went for help, returning a few hours later with several strong men.

Within a week, a house was standing on the site for Sam's

family. Because Sam was so short, the house was built to his size. Raht and his wife built a new house for themselves near Sam's house, and Raht became the founding father of the village that soon grew up around them.

Pastor Hiscox returned to the island the following week, happily surprised to see how well things had gone. He nearly bumped his head on the top of the door of Sam's house. "You are a good carpenter, Sam," he said, "but you forget that we are not all as small as you!" The pastor spent a few minutes inspecting the construction project and then turned to Sam again. "Did my friend help you get started here last week?" he asked.

"I have not yet met your friend," Sam said, and he recounted the shaky start that he and Jonathan had had on the island.

Pastor Hiscox apologized for the mix-up. "But at least everything has turned out OK," he said. "I'll go to Espíritu Santo and buy iron and nails for the roof. You press on with the school buildings, and I'll bring Norah and the children the next time I come."

The villagers on Mavea were eager to learn about Christianity. They dubbed the "Seven Days Church" as a "Clean Church." A village without pigs really made a difference. The contrast of the "clean church" village and the old ones was remarkable. Sam and Norah encouraged the people to set their houses out in rows, to plant low hedges, and to keep their places neat and tidy. They also insisted on proper sanitation and disposal of garbage.

But none of the villagers became Adventists until after a tragedy that occurred three years after Sam had arrived.

Mavea Island had been used by the Americans for bombing practice during World War II, and unexploded bombs littered the jungle. The natives had been warned to leave them alone, but some of them paid no heed to the warnings. One day the people in a nearby village put four of the unexploded bombs in the ground to support some metal screen salvaged from an airstrip, then lighted a fire under the screen to cook a large feast.

The resulting explosion killed three and injured several others.

Because Sam had medicines with him, the villagers raced to his settlement for help. Not only did he bandage up the wounds of the survivors, but he was also asked to help in the burials. The villagers were impressed with Sam's service and the Bible's promise of the resurrection. Twenty-two of them asked for Bible studies, which Sam gladly gave them, and they were then baptized.

Three years later, the Adventist Church had its largest baptism ever in the New Hebrides. On a memorable Sabbath afternoon, Sam Dick and several other pastors baptized 150 people! Pastor Dick's face beamed at the people coming toward him in the water. He was so short that he was barely able to keep his head above the waves, but he rejoiced in the victories that his God was bringing as he ministered among the people.

That evening Pastor Hiscox approached Sam. "We're very pleased with your work, Sam," he said. "And we don't want to lose you."

Sam felt puzzled. What did the mission president mean, "We don't want to lose you"? But Pastor Hiscox's next question really startled him.

"Have you and Norah ever thought of being missionaries?" the president asked.

"What do you mean, Sir?" Sam replied. "The missionaries always come to us."

The president smiled. "I know that's what you're used to," he said. "But there is a great need in New Guinea right now for someone who is closer to the culture of the people than the Australians and the Americans. They have asked if we have a native pastor here in the New Hebrides who could go to New Guinea and help them. Since you would be leaving your own homeland to work for God, you would be a missionary."

Sam shook his head. "No, Sir," he said. "I had never thought of that, and I'm sure Norah never has either."

"We felt that you are the best person we could send," Pastor Hiscox said. "Talk it over with Norah, and pray about it, and let me know what you think."

Chapter 13
Terror on the Ocean

Sam and Norah enjoyed their cruise on a passenger ship to Honiara, the capital of the Solomon Islands, but from there they had to travel on a freighter. "We'll be camping out on the deck," Sam explained gently to Norah as they discussed the second portion of their trip to New Guinea. "There are no passenger cabins on the freighter. I might find a corner to sleep in down in the crewmen's quarters, but that would leave you and the children alone on the deck, and the sailors are such a rough bunch I would not feel safe doing that."

Norah was alarmed. "The deck?" she asked in surprise. With four young children, the threat of rain, and a choppy sea, she wondered at her husband's wisdom in booking passage on a freighter. "I don't like the idea," she said, "but if that is the only way we can get to Rabaul, I guess we'll just have to do it. God will protect us, as He has before."

When they boarded the small ship, Norah noticed that the metal rods in the railing around the deck were much too far apart. She and Sam would have to watch at all times, or one large swell could send a child sprawling through the rails into the ocean. Sam selected a spot at the front of the ship where they could stay. It was right next to the cabin wall, behind the anchor rigging, and thus provided some protection from the wind.

From the time she came on board, Norah was uneasy about the sailors' advances. They leered at her, and they brushed past her even when it was not necessary. With homemade cigarettes dangling from their fingertips, some of them hung around the deck staring at her silently until the entire cigarette was finished. Never before had she felt so unsafe. Norah breathed a sigh of relief when the ship left port. Now that the sailors had work to do, they might leave her alone!

The children were hungry, so Norah pulled out the picnic supper she had prepared. Together they watched the sun go down in a brilliant arc of color on the horizon.

But the cover of darkness brought new dangers. With the ship running smoothly on course, the sailors brought out whiskey. Their laughing and shouting became louder and rougher. Norah overheard snatches of conversation from sailors roaming the deck, and what she heard made her shiver. *She* was the topic of their conversation. She was in danger!

She forced herself to stay awake. The sailors edged closer and closer, and she felt like a hunted animal. They were laughing, daring each other to touch her.

Norah curled up close to Sam, who lay sound asleep. She pressed her eyes tightly together, and soon she heard nothing. Had the sailors gone away? Thinking they had, Norah began to let herself drift off into sleep. Suddenly she awoke with a scream. One of the sailors had crept up behind her and was groping for her leg. She kicked at him and scrambled out of the way, but the sailor lunged at her.

Sam and the children were now wide awake, and the children ran to the rail to get away from the skirmish. Instantly Norah scrambled after them and started counting heads. Just then a swell lifted the boat and tipped it sideways. Norah screamed as Lawrence, her youngest son, lost his balance and dropped between the rails into the water.

"Sam! Lawrence has fallen off the ship!" Norah shouted.

"How? Where? Which side?" Sam demanded. The little ship was making about six knots—much faster than the fastest of walking speeds.

"There! There!" Norah pointed to the back of the ship.

The captain had seen the skirmish from his cabin. Immediately, he cut the engines and ordered the ship to turn around. However, to Norah it seemed useless. At the speed they were traveling, the little boy must have fallen far behind. "Why this tragedy, God?" she wondered. "We are working for you!"

Sam grabbed for a rope that hung from the side of the ship, and as he leaned over the edge he saw something dark bobbing in the water. It was Lawrence! He was crying.

"Hold on!" Sam called. "I'll pull you up."

It was not far from the water up to the deck. As soon as Lawrence's head appeared over the side of the deck, Norah reached for his shirt and helped Sam pull him to safety. They dried the boy off and helped him change into dry clothes. Exhausted, he soon fell asleep, curled up beside his three brothers, but Sam and Norah stayed awake the rest of the night.

What relief they all felt when the ship docked the next day. Sam and Norah gathered their children and their few belongings and left. Now they would experience their first airplane ride. Norah hoped it wouldn't be as frightening as the near tragedy they had just experienced!

It was a small plane, but the missionary pilot managed to get all six of them inside, along with all their luggage. In a few minutes they were airborne. Sam marveled at how lush and soft the jungle seemed from above. He realized that just as the missionaries had traded hiking through the jungles for this faster form of transportation, so the old ways of his people must give way to a new way of life in Christ.

Like an undulating green wig, the forest below followed the shape of the mountains, rising higher and higher toward the sky. The pilot warned Sam that the landing strip at the mountain village of Wapenamanda was simply a clearing on the side of the mountain. "You may think we are going to run into the mountain," he said, "but all at once you will see the brown clearing ahead. We will land uphill. The strip is short, and going uphill helps the airplane to stop more quickly."

Sam nodded, his eyes wide with wonder. "And when you take off again, do you go downhill?" he asked.

The missionary nodded. "I have to make sure the engine is running properly before I start down the airstrip, because there's no turning back. Once the plane starts down that hill, the airstrip just drops away from us, and we'll be airborne off the side of the mountain over a deep gorge."

Soon the missionary pointed to a spot on the green mountain ahead. "It's right in there," he said. "We'll buzz the village, and the people will be there to meet us and put wood behind the wheels when we stop." He chuckled. "One time they weren't quick enough, and the plane began rolling!"

Sam kept his eyes on the ground below. Sure enough, they

flew over a deep, wide gorge, and suddenly the earth was directly beneath them. All he could see was dirt and trees as the plane bounced to a stop. A mass of laughing, jostling villagers hurried to put wooden planks behind the wheels.

When the pilot cut the engines, Sam was aware of every sound—even the squeak of the door and the grate of the key as the pilot pulled it from the ignition. The frightened children cowered in their seats at the sight of the strange people.

Though Sam had grown up in a primitive village, he was shocked by what he saw. Crowds of naked men and women surrounded the plane. Sam had seen partially naked people in the villages of Malekula, but many of these people had on nothing!

One thing they did wear was huge wigs of human hair, and some of them had decorated the tops of their heads with dead birds of paradise! Many of the people had bones stuck through their noses. The men carried spears, hatchets, stone axes, and bush knives. The New Guineans were tall compared to Sam's people. They towered over his little family like giants.

"So this is New Guinea!" Sam thought. He stepped out of the plane with his usual smile and tried to talk to the crowd, but quickly discovered that they did not know his form of pidgin English. He had yet another new language to learn!

With much encouragement, the children finally crept out of the plane. Sam unloaded his things from the plane and was surprised to see the villagers pick them up and hoist them to their heads, ready to help. They walked a short distance through the jungle to the mission station. Sam and Norah's home was on a compound near the home of a white missionary family.

A day or two later, after Sam had settled his family in their new quarters, he and the other missionary, John Newman, began trekking out to the villages in John's jeep to preach to the people. The primitive mountain roads were deeply rutted from monsoon rains, and the little jeep lurched and twisted along, falling into one rut and then slamming into another. Rounding a corner, they suddenly came face-to-face with a wall of mud—a landslide across the road. Just then a group of men came walking down the road. Pastor Newman climbed out of the jeep and offered to pay them for their help. With eager smiles they took the shovels he handed them, cleared the road, and in no time, it seemed, the jeep was on its way.

The next obstacle was a river. There was a bridge of sorts across it. Two logs had been laid across the river, parallel to each other. The bridge builders had flattened the top surface of each log, but Sam worried about what would happen if the natural shape of the logs did not match the tires. Would they fall into the river and be swept downstream? He soon got his answer. Pastor Newman started across the bridge, with Sam standing behind to verify that the logs were spaced correctly for the tires. Everything seemed OK. Closer and closer the jeep inched to the middle of the bridge. Sam watched nervously, whispering a prayer.

All at once, with a resounding crack, one of the wheels slipped off of its log, and the jeep was straddling the bridge with Pastor Newman balanced precariously inside. Before Sam had time to think what to do next, a cheery band of villagers appeared, and for a small fee they hoisted the jeep back onto the logs with much cheering and shouting. Soon Sam was walking across the logs to join Pastor Newman.

But if he thought the jeep bridge was bad, he was petrified at the sight of the footbridge they came to at the end of the road. This "bridge" was nothing more than vines twisted together and strung across the gorge, suspended from a rope of wire and twisted vines above it. It was New Guinea's version of the Golden Gate Bridge!

Sam watched Pastor Newman start across. At first he was able to hold on to the suspension vines, but near the center of the bridge these supporting vines joined the bridge itself, and there was nothing above to hang on to! Sam held his breath till Pastor Newman had made it across the center section; then he sat down and slowly made his way across the gorge.

But even that experience paled when, on a later trip, Pastor Newman took Sam across a swaying, vine-suspension bridge in the jeep! Sam was not sure whether he would live to tell about it, but fortunately they made it to the other side in spite of their weak knees and churning stomachs.

It was no wonder the people of New Guinea knew less about God than Sam's own father, Ool. They were so isolated that few missionaries had dared penetrate their jungle.

One of the villages, Laiagam, was up in the mountains 9,000 feet above sea level. A heavy frost gripped the village each night. Feeling sorry for the people who lived in these primitive conditions, the missionaries brought blankets to help them keep warm. However, the villagers had devised their own ingenious ways to keep warm. Some of them beat strips of bark to make capes. Others lighted fires under the sleeping platforms of their houses. Still others heated stones and carried them around wrapped in bark fiber. Or, lacking stones, they would simply find a grunting pig and cuddle up next to it! As a result of these methods, the people suffered from burns and skin diseases, as well as dysentery from their unclean surroundings.

"Pay back" dominated inter-village relationships. Any wrong done to a person, family, or village must have appropriate revenge. Tribes, clans, and villages waged continual warfare. They ambushed each other, betrayed each other, knifed, speared, and axed each other. Sam spent many hours trying to head off fights, patch up quarrels, and teach Christian love and courtesy.

When he preached, Sam's main attention-getting device was a red gramophone—what he called a "finga fone." It was a miniature record player operated with a finger hole on the turntable. Sam put a disc on the turntable, poked his finger in the finger hole, and spun the turntable. The natives were amazed to hear a voice in their own dialect coming from the little red box! Whenever Sam entered a village and set his little "finga fone" down, crowds of villagers surrounded him to see his "magic."

Of course, with his "gift of tongues," in a day or two Sam could have preached a sermon in the native dialect, but the finga fone so captured the villagers' attention that he chose to let it do the preaching instead. Soon Adventist villages were springing up all over that part of New Guinea.

Because he looked more like themselves, the natives accepted Sam more readily than they did the white missionaries. Nevertheless, Sam and Norah were lonely. The Newmans had memories of Australia and Avondale College to share with the visitors who flew in from time to time, but none of them could reminisce with Sam and Norah about Aore College. In the New Hebrides, Sam and Norah had eaten yams and taro, cassava and rice. But nobody grew rice in New Guinea. So Sam and Norah ate endless quantities of the local sweet potato and little else.

The loneliness burdened Norah the most. Sam wondered if they had done the right thing by coming to New Guinea.

Chapter 14
Jimmy and the Knife

Norah was pregnant again. In order to provide her with better medical care, the mission moved the Dick family to a mission station that was closer to civilization—near a town called Sopas, where the church operated a hospital.

Ironically, in the New Hebrides Norah had brought her children into the world in some of the most primitive surroundings in the world, while in undeveloped New Guinea she bore her seventh child in a hospital. Yet that stay in the hospital nearly cost her her life!

They named this son Nathan, which means "gift of God." The day Nathan was born Sam went home rejoicing, but a few days later word reached him that Norah was not doing well and could not feed the baby. He took the baby home and fed it with a bottle, leaving Norah in the hospital to recover a few more days.

At last the doctor called to say that Norah could go home—to die. Sam's heart was heavy. What would he do with seven motherless children?

Pastor and Mrs. Alec Campbell, who had spent thirty-six years in mission service, offered to look after Norah and the baby. The six older children missed their mother terribly. James, the second-oldest, seemed to be the most upset. He wondered what he could do to show his sorrow.

Soon after arriving in New Guinea, Jimmy had noticed that many men and boys had their little finger missing.

"What happened to your little finger?" Jimmy had asked one of them.

"That's for my father who died," he said.

"I cut mine off when my brother was killed in a fight," replied another.

One day, after visiting his mother, Jimmy went into the kitchen and found a sharp butcher knife. Going back into his mother's room, he found that she was still breathing, so he put the knife away. The next day when he came to see his mother, he was told that she was much worse. Sneaking into the kitchen, he again lifted the knife out of the drawer, and again he tiptoed into his mother's room to see if she had died. She hadn't, so he put the knife away again.

Everyone was so concerned about Norah that nobody noticed Jimmy coming into her room with a knife in his hand each day, ready to amputate his little finger the minute he heard she had died.

One afternoon Pastor Campbell offered to anoint Norah. "The doctors can do nothing," he told Sam. "Only God can prolong her life now."

Jimmy slipped into the room clutching the knife just as Pastor Campbell began his prayer. He watched the missionary rub some olive oil on Norah's forehead as he asked for special healing. Everyone was silent when he finished his prayer. They all watched Norah's shallow breathing with anxious hearts. Sam's lips moved as he prayed silently.

A few minutes later Norah opened her eyes and looked around the room. Then she asked for food. It was the first time she had spoken to anyone in several days! Immediately food was brought, and a prayer of thanksgiving went up to God.

It was then that Sam noticed Jimmy holding the knife. "What are you doing with that?" he asked in alarm.

Jimmy told him. The Campbells were so moved that they gave Jimmy the knife as a token of God's healing power. For many years, Sam and Norah showed the knife and told of God's miraculous healing for Norah that day in New Guinea.

Norah went home and recovered slowly but steadily. Sam and Pastor Campbell resumed their journeys into the jungle villages. One day Pastor Campbell told Sam that he wanted to climb a 10,000 foot mountain that loomed over the area, and he invited Sam to join him. Sam eagerly agreed.

They started out early one morning. The air was crystal clear as they battled their way to the top. They hoped to arrive before the sun scorched them. Sam noticed that the climb wasn't easy for the sixty-year-old missionary, but they kept a steady pace and reached the top before noon. From that vantage point the view below was superb. Across the valley, far off to the east, Mount Wilhelm's snow-capped peak pierced the clouds at a height of over 14,700 feet. Turning the other way, they could see other mountain peaks also disappear into the clouds.

Sam found breathing difficult, and he was cold. Pastor Campbell told him that he was standing higher than the plane had flown when he had first arrived in New Guinea. They rested awhile amid the wild beauty, and Pastor Campbell pointed out various areas in the valley where Adventist villages had formed. He described the sacred houses of the Sepik River to the north, where crude and obscene idols lurked in dark corners. Yet mission stations now lined the river as the Adventist missionaries pressed farther and farther inland, bringing light to the heathen villages.

Sam shook his head in amazement at what God had done. He felt particularly awed that he should be among those privileged to carry the gospel to these primitive people. Yet a glance at the vast area stretched out before them told him that there was so much left to do—so many people yet to tell! Sam's people had once been heathen, and many still were, but because of the courage of the missionaries, he now had a much happier way of life. And now he was sharing that happiness with others.

Going back down the mountain seemed easy enough. Sam led the way, and Pastor Campbell followed. Just before they reached the town of Sopas, Pastor Campbell called out, "Sam! Help me!"

Sam looked back to see Pastor Campbell slump to the ground. The color seemed drained from his body. Though the missionary was a tall man, and Sam only a little more than four feet tall, he managed to drag the white missionary along the trail until he found helpers to carry him into town. From there he hired a jeep to drive them home.

Pastor Campbell had suffered a severe stroke. He and his wife were rushed by plane to Australia, leaving Sam alone in charge of the Campbell's house and the mission property. It was a particularly difficult time, since a new addition was being built to the Sopas Adventist Hospital, and Pastor Campbell had been in charge of the project.

A few days later, a missionary from the conference came to check on how things were going. Though he still mourned the loss of Pastor Campbell, who had become like a father to him, Sam greeted the man cheerfully.

The missionary from the conference knew that Pastor Campbell had nearly $2,000 in cash somewhere in his house, and knowing that it would be some months before a replacement could come, he thought he would pick it up before it got stolen. He began by checking the pastor's office and similar logical places. Finding nothing, he examined all the furniture in the house, the locks—even the faucets! But he found nothing. Finally, with a serious face, he came to see Sam.

"Sam, come outside with me," he said. "Bring Norah and the children outside with you, but leave everything inside just as it is."

"Why, Sir? What's the problem?" Sam asked in bewilderment as he followed the missionary outside. He motioned for Norah and the children to follow.

Outside, the missionary explained. "Pastor Campbell had a lot of money in cash. I can't find it, and much as I don't want to suspect you of taking it, Sam, I must go into your house and look through your things. You are the only one with a key to the house."

A sudden warm flush came to Sam's cheeks and spread throughout his body. Norah tensed beside him. Though they knew they'd done nothing wrong, they both felt terribly ashamed, for in their culture shame is an emotion felt more often than guilt. Shame overwhelms a person when he is falsely accused or when a higher official fails to show trust and respect. What could Sam say when the white man could not find the money? How could he defend himself? It would be just the white man's word against his.

Sam also wondered what this sudden turn of events would do to his career as a worker for the Lord. Would they fire him? Two thousand dollars was more than he earned in a whole year! At last Sam found his voice. "Money isn't new to me, Sir," he said. "During the war I collected all the tithes and offerings for nearly half of the New Hebrides. And though I had only a second-grade education, I knew how to keep track of the money and turn it over to the mission. I have had far more than $2,000 in my hands several times."

"Nevertheless, the money is gone, and you have the key, Sam," the missionary said.

"Sir, no one has ever asked me about a sixpence, or even one penny. I have never been suspected of robbing from God's storehouse! I would never do a thing like that!"

"But you have the key," the missionary said again. He shook his head and ran a frustrated hand through his hair. "I don't know what to think."

Sam gave permission. While he and Norah waited shamefully outside their house, the missionary went inside and searched through everything. He did not find the money, and he left that afternoon with a heavy heart, hoping Sam was not a thief, but still a little suspicious, wondering why the money had just disappeared.

Sam and Norah spent several agonizing days searching the missionary's house for the money. They hadn't even known it was there until the missionary from the conference told them. It was just gone! How could they be held responsible for taking care of something they didn't know existed? Because of his stroke, Pastor Campbell could not tell anyone what he had done with the money. What would happen to them now?

On Monday a man came knocking at the door. "I have come to pay tithe on the money I earned cutting lumber for the new addition to the Sopas Hospital," he said.

Sam didn't want to hear any more about money, but he went for the receipt book. Counting out the money—fifteen shillings—he started to write a receipt, then sat back in surprise. "You have already paid fifteen shillings in tithe!" he exclaimed. "Here in the book is the receipt for it." He held the receipt book up for the man to see.

The man shook his head. "That is a different fifteen shillings. I brought lumber to Sopas two weeks ago for the hospital. The first fifteen shillings tithe is from what I earned at that time. Today I brought more lumber, and this is the tithe on that."

In a flash, Sam understood what had happened. "Did Pastor Campbell pay you in advance to cut those logs?" he asked.

The man nodded.

"Then you sold the logs and are returning the tithe from that sale?"

Again the man nodded.

"How much money did Pastor Campbell give you?"

The man told him, and Sam wrote down the amount. "Did Pastor Campbell pay anyone else to cut logs?" he asked.

The man began to reel off the names.

"Could you spread the word that I want to see them all?" Sam said fervently.

One by one the lumber cutters came to see Sam, and he wrote down the name of each man and the amount Pastor Campbell had given him. Then he took the list to Sopas and checked with the builder to be sure that the figures were correct and that the men were actually bringing cut lumber for the building.

Sam totaled the money. It came to almost exactly $2,000! He and Norah breathed a sigh of relief. Now, if the missionary would believe them, they could be rid of their shame.

Before long the missionary made another surprise visit. Still suspicious that Sam might have stolen the money and hidden it somewhere, he looked around for signs of any purchases that Sam and Norah might have made with their new-found "wealth" as he walked into their house, but he saw nothing.

Sam welcomed the missionary happily. "Sir!" he said. "I have the most good news for you! I have found the money—or at least I know where it has gone."

Sam produced the list that he had so painstakingly made. After studying it, the missionary's face broke into a slow smile. "Well, I'm happy, Sam. And I'm sorry for the misunderstanding."

Sam nodded. "Then I will not lose my job?"

"You have found where the money went," the missionary said. "I'm sure you will have many more years of service to the Lord."

Norah touched her husband's arm tenderly, and they smiled at each other. She had known all along that Sam could be trusted!

Chapter 15
Mouth of the CHIEF

Norah had been ill for some time. Because she was not getting well, Sam asked the mission if he could return home to the New Hebrides. "I've been here in New Guinea four years now," he told the committee. "My wife has been very ill, and the doctor doesn't think she should stay here any longer. My children must return and learn to live in their own country. My son Jonathan is nearly finished at Aore and is ready to be a preacher. I know they'll have something for me back in the New Hebrides."

Sam and Nora were transferred back to the New Hebrides, and soon Norah was well and strong again.

And sure enough, the mission there did have something in mind for Sam. "We want you to go to Port Stanley as district director," the mission president said.

"How big is that district?"

"You'll have charge of the work on Malekula, Paama, Ambrim, Epi, and Mahe."

Sam knew that the work had grown in his absence. "How many pastors and teachers are there in the district?" he asked.

"At the moment there are more than twenty paid workers and many who work for the church full time without pay. We have fifteen locations where there are schools and churches. You'll have your hands full!"

Sam marveled at the twists and turns his life had taken. One missionary wondered about his honesty with Pastor Campbell's money. And then he was given the largest assignment in the mission—a responsibility that would require his handling thousands of dollars!

That night Sam and Norah had a special prayer together.

"Thank You, Lord, for healing Norah, for helping us to find that money, and for giving us souls for our work in New Guinea. Now go with us in this big new job You have given us to do."

Sam, the little baby God had saved for His purposes, finally returned to his home island. Sam's beloved Malekula welcomed him as God's talking chief. No longer was he "mouth of the chief" but "mouth of the CHIEF"—God! Big and Little Nambus people came to the church. Sam felt happier than he had ever been before.

Most touching of all was the day Alma Wiles returned to the spot on Malua Bay where she had buried her husband, Norman, some forty years before. She stood by his grave and wept as she thought of the past, but she did not weep for long. Around her gathered old men who remembered her and her husband, and who now shared her faith in God.

Hundreds came to see her during her brief visit to the island. When she left the island alone forty years before, following her husband's tragic death, she had no idea what results their witness would bring. She had been discouraged then. Her husband's death had seemed so useless.

But when she returned, she found thousands of Adventists who counted her and her husband as their spiritual parents. It was almost like being in heaven. If only Norman could have known the results of his work! Sam told her how much he appreciated the work she and the Smiths had done and assured her that God had worked through them to bring him to Christianity. Sam was thankful that God had chosen to use Norman to win others as well.

In 1960 Sam came home to Aore, the strategic hub of the Adventist work in the New Hebrides. To his dismay, he found the school in a state of chaos. It was not a happy place to be. Longstanding arguments about diet made both students and teachers unhappy. Some wanted to prohibit any meat from being served at the school, even though there was no other affordable source of protein which the students would eat. The teachers were becoming discouraged, and many wanted to leave.

As if that were not enough, a wave of enthusiasm about the second coming of Jesus had swept through the Adventist community. At first everyone rejoiced in the sureness of Christ's soon return, but fanaticism caught hold, and the students refused to plant fresh coconuts in the aging copra plantation because the coconuts would never be ready to harvest before the Lord came. Others questioned the need for any new buildings. Sam had helped to build the school and didn't want to see it hurt. Fortunately, the situation improved within two months after he arrived.

Sam had also helped to build the Aore Adventist Hospital. Now he set about to draw the workers together in a common goal. With his compassion and concern, he succeeded in improving morale among the hospital staff and patients. He could speak just about every language of the islands and frequently acted as interpreter for the patients.

Even the diet problem was eventually resolved. The dietitians worked out a vegetarian diet which the students could approve. Soon the school embarked on a coconut-planting program that eventually renewed the copra (dried coconut meat) harvest. The new cocoa plantation added to the financial prospects for the school.

For the next seven years Sam lived the busy life of an administrator: preaching, organizing, settling church problems, staffing the mission settlements—the work seemed endless!

Sam's dedication to his people was obvious. At one meeting of the hospital committee, a doctor was pressing for the addition of a new tuberculosis ward. Reasons piled up why the hospital couldn't afford a ward for TB patients only. No money. No staff. Infection might spread. Most of all—*NO MONEY*

Sam had heard it all before, and as the hours passed, he grew more and more impatient with the reasoning. A man with a prayer vine linking him to Heaven's resources could hardly accept such arguments. "All I hear is, 'no money, no money, no money!' " he protested at last. "Don't you know who owns the money of the world? You white men don't have to worry. You get sick, and the church flies you home to our hospital in Sydney. But what about my people? Who will care for them if they get sick? They don't have a hospital, and they're dying.

"Where's your faith?" he asked. "Why don't you trust God? If He wants us to have a hospital, He will provide."

Sam's reasoning ended the argument. The committee voted that day to build a TB ward and to ask the people in Australia to help. Sam Dick was thrilled. After all, besides being pastor, he was still talking chief for the CHIEF.

Within two years the hospital had a TB ward, and Sam had new responsibilities as dean of boys, senior church pastor, and general advisor to the school. He still could not read well, but his influence was strong. However, his lack of education did not dampen his enthusiasm for Christian education. He saw the Adventist schools as a door through which his people could walk to a better life. On committees, and wherever he could get a hearing, he urged his missionary comrades to build more and better schools.

Because of Sam's influence, family unity became more apparent in the church. Sam had read in Ellen White's books that it was God's will that families should sit together in church. This was difficult for new Adventists to accept in the New Hebrides. In their culture, women ranked lower than a healthy pig. Men felt ashamed to be seen with women in a public place! So in church, some of the men sat together without their wives, while others followed Sam's example of sitting with their entire families. Many wives asked their husbands, "Why don't you treat me like Sam Dick treats Norah?"

But the status of women was not the most serious problem at Aore. In 1980, changes within the government began to threaten the very existence of the school that Sam had helped to build. The New Hebrides had long been under English domination. Now the nationals wanted independence. They no longer wanted to be called "New Hebrides"—a name plucked by someone's vivid imagination from a group of islands off the coast of Scotland. Now people were speaking of *Vanuatu*, "our land."

A French survey team came to check the properties on Aore. Anyone who could not establish his survey details would lose his property. Confidently, Sam Dick walked the boundary with the survey team, pointing out markers that he had placed as a teenager years before, and locating them on a survey map of the island. Reluctantly the team confirmed that the Adventists had rights to their land.

Chapter 16
"I Shall Stay at Aore!"

The political situation made it unsafe for the Australian missionaries to stay at Aore, so the decision was made to move their offices to another island. The atmosphere around the school was one of chaos again, as the missionaries packed up their most valuable belongings and loaded them into the mission boat for a quick trip across the strait.

When they returned for more of their things, they were met at the dock by gun-carrying officers who refused to let them get out of the boat. The missionaries pleaded for permission to get just a few more things, but when the guns clicked, they became silent. They reversed the little ship and left the dock at gunpoint.

Sam and the other native teachers were now threatened. Every morning a radio news broadcaster, aiming his words directly at them, screamed, "Look out, Aore, today we are coming to get you. Get off the island while there is still time. We got rid of your white leaders. Now we'll get rid of you!"

The staff and students began to panic. Some talked about leaving. Sam worried what would happen if everyone left the school. He knew that vandals would strip the place of everything that was movable, and squatters would move in and establish their right to live on the property. The coconut plantation would be neglected. The school and hospital that Sam had helped build would be destroyed. He could think of no worse blow to God's work!

One night he talked the situation over with Norah. They could easily return to Malekula, for he still had land rights at Bartarmul. There were other places, too, where they could flee, but they decided to stay at Aore. The stubborn streak that had characterized their lives was still evident.

In staff meeting the next morning, Sam announced, "I know some of you have discussed leaving Aore. I want to tell you that Norah and I are *not* leaving. You can all go, but we're staying!" He looked around the group solemnly, his jaw set.

"You might get killed!" the other teachers protested. "What if the police come? Or what if the prime minister sends the soldiers from New Guinea? We're just not safe here."

"We don't need to fear men," replied the man who had stood up to similar opposition in the past. "We have God on our side! Trust God. He will look after us." Then Sam began to tell the story of his life. He told about the shining white angels that protected the missionary's home when he and his family were still heathen cannibals. He told of the time he and his family were forced out of their home on the island of Paama and taken to a prison in Tavie, and of the British officer who set them free. And he told how, instead of being forced by that same British officer to work on the Sabbath, God arranged for him to be appointed pastor over *all* the churches on Paama. "I am a part of God's plan for Vanuatu," Sam said confidently. "He will not let me down. He built Aore. He will not let Satan destroy it now."

The younger teachers exchanged uneasy looks. How could they let this "old man" stay alone at Aore?

A voice called out, "If Sam is staying, so am I."

Soon another voice said, "I'm staying too."

One by one, others joined these leaders. And so it was that when all the other schools in the area closed and the staff and students scattered to islands near and far, Aore—the Adventist center—remained open. When the unrest was over, the missionaries returned and resumed their work. The prestige of the school and the church was never higher than at that time.

In 1980 the biggest thrill of his life came when Pastor Sam Dick was named as a delegate to the General Conference session in Dallas, Texas. Now he would see the land that an American soldier had told him years ago was "the other heaven."

Sam marveled at the masses of people running "to and fro" on the highways and at the expansive stores with so much to buy. On Sabbath morning, as he was riding in a car along a busy freeway, Sam commented, "How nice it is. All these people are going to church with us!"

When he was told that the cars on the freeway were zooming along to a thousand different destinations, Sam was amazed. "In the jungle," he said, "when you meet someone walking the same direction, you know you are going to the same place. Each trail goes to one place in one direction and to another place in the other direction. In America life is too fast!"

Most of all, Sam marveled at how unhappy many Americans are. "This is not the other heaven," he said. "It's just like Vanuatu. People here are sick and lonely and frightened, just like where I come from. They don't know about God's love any more than many of the people on my islands. They are just like my people in the jungles. There's no place like heaven but heaven itself."

Sam returned to Vanuatu a thankful man. He retired in 1981 on the Island of Malo, near Aore, but he still helps out whenever called to be dean of boys or pastor or peacemaker to warring tribes. During Sam's lifetime, the Adventist church in Vanuatu grew from zero to over 6,000 members! Of his incredible climb from heathen baby to Adventist minister, Pastor Dick says, "Whenever I had a problem, I didn't turn to people. I didn't try to fight my way out. I turned to God. God made me strong to do His work. I prayed to Him. I was connected to Him as if a vine reached from heaven to me. With Him at my side, I could win any battle."